"on the subject of the *feminist* business"

PETER LANG
New York • Washington, D.C./Baltimore • Bern
Frankfurt am Main • Berlin • Brussels • Vienna • Oxford

"on the subject of the *feminist* business"

re-reading flannery o'connor

EDITED BY
Teresa Caruso

PETER LANG
New York • Washington, D.C./Baltimore • Bern
Frankfurt am Main • Berlin • Brussels • Vienna • Oxford

Library of Congress Cataloging-in-Publication Data

"On the subject of the feminist business":
re-reading Flannery O'Connor / edited by Teresa Caruso.
p. cm.
Includes bibliographical references and index.
1. O'Connor, Flannery—Criticism and interpretation. 2. Feminism and literature—Southern States—History—20th century. 3. Women and literature—Southern States—History—20th century. 4. Feminist fiction, American—History and criticism. I. Caruso, Teresa.
PS3565.C57Z815 813'.54—dc22 2003027813
ISBN 0-8204-7149-6

Bibliographic information published by **Die Deutsche Bibliothek**.
Die Deutsche Bibliothek lists this publication in the "Deutsche Nationalbibliografie"; detailed bibliographic data is available on the Internet at http://dnb.ddb.de/.

Cover design by Dutton & Sherman Design

The paper in this book meets the guidelines for permanence and durability of the Committee on Production Guidelines for Book Longevity of the Council of Library Resources.

275 Seventh Avenue, 28th Floor, New York, NY 10001
www.peterlangusa.com

Printed in the United States of America

With special thanks to

Joe Caruso

Greg Morris

Celise Schneider

Dean Baldwin

Dan Frankforter

Ron Emerick

Gayle Morris

Peggy Wilfong

Contents

Acknowledgments

The contributors to this book gratefully acknowledge permission to reprint the following:

From *The Feminine Mystique* by Betty Friedan. Copyright © 1983, 1974, 1973, 1963 by Betty Friedan. Used by permission of W. W. Norton & Company, Inc.

Excerpts from "A Good Man is Hard to Find" and "The Life You Save May Be Your Own" in *A Good Man is Hard to Find and Other Stories,* copyright 1953 by Flannery O'Connor and renewed 1981 by Regina O'Connor, reprinted by permission of Harcourt, Inc.

Excerpts from "A Temple of the Holy Ghost" in *A Good Man is Hard to Find and Other Stories,* copyright 1954 by Flannery O'Connor and renewed 1982 by Regina O'Connor, reprinted by permission of Harcourt, Inc.

Excerpts from "Good Country People" in *A Good Man is Hard to Find and Other Stories,* copyright © 1955 by Flannery O'Connor and renewed 1983 by Regina O'Connor, reprinted by permission of Harcourt, Inc.

Excerpt from "A Circle in the Fire" in *A Good Man is Hard to Find and Other Stories,* copyright 1948 by Flannery O'Connor and renewed 1976 by Mrs. Edward F. O'Connor, reprinted by permission of Harcourt, Inc.

Excerpts from *The Complete Stories* by Flannery O'Connor. Copyright © 1971 by the Estate of Mary Flannery O'Connor. Reprinted by permission of Farrar, Straus and Giroux, LLC.

Excerpts from *Everything That Rises Must Converge* by Flannery O'Connor. Copyright © 1965 by the Estate of Mary Flannery O'Connor. Copyright renewed 1993 by Regina O'Connor. Reprinted by permission of Farrar, Straus and Giroux, LLC.

Excerpts from *The Habit of Being: Letters of Flannery O'Connor* edited by Sally Fitzgerald. Copyright © 1979 by Regina O'Connor. Reprinted by permission of Farrar, Straus and Giroux, LLC.

Excerpts from *Mystery and Manners* by Flannery O'Connor. Copyright © 1969 by the Estate of Mary Flannery O'Connor. Reprinted by permission of Farrar, Straus and Giroux, LLC.

Excerpts from *Wise Blood* by Flannery O'Connor. Copyright © 1962 by Flannery O'Connor. Copyright renewed © 1990 by Regina O'Connor. Reprinted by permission of Farrar, Straus and Giroux, LLC.

Introduction: "On the subject of the feminist business"

TERESA CARUSO

Critics have long relied on Flannery O'Connor's own statements when approaching her work; since she emphasized the spiritual nature of her writing, the bulk of O'Connor criticism to date focuses on the Christian elements of her fiction, subjects that include original sin, the mystery of grace and redemption, the fear of God. In keeping with O'Connor's stated purpose for writing what she did, the way she did, scholars have offered little in the way of feminist criticism. Those critics who do offer a more specifically feminist approach to O'Connor's work often subjugate feminism to theology or other avenues of approach. While O'Connor's spiritual stance certainly offers a valid and fertile basis for theological criticism, for many readers these theological interpretations have long failed to afford complete (or, I would argue, satisfactory) understanding of her stories (Westling 520). We run the risk of lessening the import of O'Connor's work by offering no multiplicity of readings. O'Connor believed that "the intentions of the writer have to be found in the work itself" because "a work of art exists without its author from the moment the words are on paper" (*Mystery and Manners* 126), and she was well aware of the possibility of multiple angles of vision, multiple interpretations from her readers, as evidenced by comments in her letters: "Perhaps you are able to see things in these stories that I can't see because if I did see I would be too frightened to write them" (*Habit of Being* 149). O'Connor also realized that her stories were not always composed of things intended: "I certainly have no idea how I have written about some of the things I have, as they are things I am not conscious of having thought about one way or the other" (*Habit of Being* 180), an admission that should serve to dismiss any reluctance on the part of critics to approach O'Connor's work from a feminist vantage point simply because of her claims to have no affinity with or conscious thought about "the subject of the feminist business" (*Habit of Being* 176).

In addition to the critical reticence created by O'Connor's own beliefs and statements, the historical neglect of her work by feminists may also result from O'Connor's subject matter. Feminist criticism demonstrates the existence of certain preoccupations and techniques in women's writing, many of which are embedded in social and cultural constructions (Humm 198). One of those preoccupations is the preponderance of domesticity in setting and other thematic elements, since women's texts often revolve around the home. O'Connor's stories do contain domestic settings, but she does not "follow the rules" in that her stories rarely involve the typical female milieu of the household and its activities. Furthermore, her tales certainly trigger what has often been considered as a negative result of feminist criticism: the portrayal of woman as victim. No doubt an author who routinely wounds, cripples, shoots, and gores her female characters invites some measure of perceived betrayal from feminist readers. Yet, the concept of woman as universal victim can be positive if victimization and oppression are clearly understood. Recognizing woman as exploited and dominated does not necessarily place her in the status of "victim" since feminist scholarship can also provide a key as to how power works (Sorisio 143). Since our understanding of the term "victim" is a cultural construct, internalized by men and women (even those who are victimized), victimization can be understood in social contexts and in "gender relations" (Lamb 3).

Flannery O'Connor's women provide perfect examples of social and cultural victimization, specifically manifested through her use of the grotesque. Marshall Bruce Gentry notes that in O'Connor's fiction, the grotesque relies upon an "ideal [that] can be inferred from its degraded form...and this ideal provides the standard by which a character is to be understood" (10–11). The disfigured, dismembered and abnormal bodies in O'Connor's fiction distinctly contrast with the (inferred) ideal body, but the grotesquerie of her characters stems from more than their physical features. The spiritual truths revealed to O'Connor's characters through their epiphanies allow the reader to understand both the characters and the religious ideals from which they deviate. However, for the "resisting reader" (see Fetterley), these truths differ for male and female characters in that those truths revealed to her females are not always clearly theological and do not always clearly relate to O'Connor's stated religious purpose—resulting in a "feminine grotesque" that asserts itself as a "gender issue" (Reesman 40). The grotesquerie of O'Connor's female characters emanates not only from a degradation of religious or spiritual ideals, but also (and perhaps more so) through their declination from cultural or social ideals, particularly those concerning constructs of the paragon of (Southern) womanhood and woman's place in society.

A close examination of Flannery O'Connor's work indicates that her women, even those without face or voice who haunt the backgrounds of her stories, are imprisoned within a culture that defines female only in opposition to male, a society that values its women only for their duty to men. O'Connor's women are, in some manner, effectively silenced or subject to erasure—those women who are given a voice are nevertheless silenced in that they do not speak with authority. O'Connor's women are powerless in the face of the patriarchy that controls them, a control that extends beyond the merely physical into the unconscious, manipulating their actions and rendering them grotesque in ways that do not affect O'Connor's males. Moreover, a lack of strong (self-) identity often accompanies this powerlessness. The fact that many of O'Connor's women are nameless has not gone unnoticed. Innumerable references have been made to the unnamed mothers of Julian in "Everything That Rises Must Converge," Thomas in "The Comforts of Home," and Bailey in "A Good Man Is Hard to Find." These particular women are joined by a host of others who exist in the backgrounds of O'Connor's stories, some named, some not. Although their presence has been noted, the women themselves have gone largely unnoticed. While Richard Giannone claims that "[n]owhere in O'Connor's work do we find women dramatized in…the repeated literary state of 'simulacrum, erasure, or silence'" (74), O'Connor's stories are, in fact, full of silent and invisible women. Readers and critics alike have dismissed or overlooked many of O'Connor's women because they are silent or barely visible in the background of the stories—and those women whose presence cannot be ignored have gone unsympathized, even when they may have deserved our sympathies.

The resisting reader sees these women in a new light, sympathizing with those who have not previously gained readers' compassions, and hearing those who may be silent—or silenced—for "silence is nothing more or less than what lies outside the radius of interest and comprehension at any given time. We hear…with culturally attuned ears" (Retallack 345). We also read with culturally attuned minds and must remain aware that "silence is not empty at all, but densely, richly, disturbingly full. Full of just those things which we had not, until 'now,' been ready to notice; or reluctantly noticing, had dismissed as nonsense or noise" (Retallack 345). The resisting reader enters the text, looks for the "presence of absence" (Shands 73) in order to re-create the female text to discern the *real* presence of the women in O'Connor's work. Without such resistance, readers risk being drawn into understanding O'Connor's female characters through those cultural (male) ideals presented as acceptable by a patriarchal society. Such risk increases with O'Connor's work because of her unfailing ability to see and to accurately record the world around her, a responsibility she insisted fell to any author. In "Writing Short Stories," O'Connor tells would-be writers that "[y]our beliefs will be the light by which you see, but they will not be what you see" (*Mystery and Manners* 91). Writing about *what* she sees, O'Connor draws her women from something more concrete than the religious beliefs through which her vision filters. The women she writes about are real women immersed in the strong patriarchal society of the South, women who form an integral part of the culture that produces and defines that society.

O'Connor's work remains problematic for many readers, since just as she refuses to provide specific theological direction in her work, the texts of her stories provide no satisfactory resolutions to feminist issues. Yet there are issues at stake in O'Connor's work that should concern the feminist reader—even those who may be reluctant to approach O'Connor because she does not offer what is expected of a woman writer. Rather than allowing O'Connor's "failure" to create dominant female characters to shut down her works by assuming her recalcitrance to speak directly against the patriarchy to be inadvertent or misogynistic, feminist readers can and should use O'Connor's difference to open up new approaches. In his introduction to *Flannery O'Connor: New Perspectives* (1996), Sura Rath provides a comprehensive history of O'Connor criticism, noting the absence of feminist approaches that would create a fresh line of inquiry into her work. More recently, in *Revising Flannery O'Connor* (2001), Kathleen Hemple Prown explores some possible reasons for that absence, but critics have thus far failed to provide an examination of O'Connor's work from a distinctly feminist point of view. The essays collected here begin to fulfill this need for mainstream feminist approaches to O'Connor's work.

Robert Donahoo questions the judgments of early feminist critics who view Flannery O'Connor's women as manifestations of the author's own internalized cultural misogyny. Juxtaposing O'Connor's female character depictions with the real-life female subjects studied by Betty Friedan in *The Feminine Mystique*, Donahoo finds that many of O'Connor's portrayals and much of her social criticism parallel situations recounted by Friedan, and suggests that O'Connor was not a victim of her culture, but a visionary for women's issues.

Similarly, Virginia Wray tracks the changes in O'Connor's female protagonists from her early, unpublished writings to "Revelation," defending O'Connor from charges of misogyny by positing that the later characters successfully subvert the open rebellion of the young protagonists found in the earlier sketches, until openly reappearing once again in the book-throwing Mary Grace.

Several of these essays provide new readings of both O'Connor's stories and O'Connor criticism. Margaret D. Bauer re-reads "A Stroke of Good Fortune" and "Good Country People" and re-views the body of criticism dealing with these stories from a feminist perspective, considering Ruby Hill and Joy-Hulga as more sympathetic characters than previously found. Bauer reads O'Connor's texts as exemplifying the punishment that awaits those who attempt to thwart the patriarchy, rather than as a demonstration of O'Connor's own alliance with patriarchal conventions.

Marshall Bruce Gentry also responds to previous readings, including his own, of "A View of the Woods." Gentry approaches O'Connor's text through the lens of German psychologist Alice Miller, re-reading it not as the old man's story, but as the story of the young girl and a critique of the patriarchy in which she lives that imposes silence and violence upon its females.

Dawn Keetley foregrounds such violence in her reading of "A Good Man Is Hard to Find." Keetley reads the second part of the story as the Grandmother's fantasy, her dream of escape from the oppressive restraints of a familial/social structure that devalues women in general, old women in particular. The Grandmother's desire to act, to assert herself and to create her own identity informs an awareness that she has violated social mores; her offense, untenable in a strong, Southern patriarchy, causes her to inflict her own punishment on the transgressive body.

The female body as a site of contestation informs other essays here as well. Natalie Wilson approaches O'Connor's work from a corporeal feminist perspective, reading her stories as a feminist critique of the social and cultural entrapment that fosters violence against the female, particularly the female body. These cultural norms, internalized and upheld by females, depicted through inferior, abnormal, unacceptable bodies contrast with the "normal" body of patriarchy that warps both men and women.

Christine Atkins reads "Good Country People" as a rape-script that overrides the script of Joy-Hulga's fantasy of seduction, demonstrating that Joy-Hulga's violation points to women's lack of self-control (over body and mind) and the violence often associated with the coming-of-age experience for females, particularly those who fail to adhere to patriarchal norms.

Avis Hewitt reads "A View of the Woods" as an indicator of the domination of man over land, the land as female and Mary Fortune Pitts as the ground over which Pitts and Old Man Fortune battle. Mary Fortune, as an embodiment of the land, is a body to be conquered. Old Man Fortune wants her to conform to his will just as he wishes to conform the land to his dreams of progress—and destroys her just as he wishes to destroy the land.

Finally, as Jody June Schade notes in the conclusion, O'Connor may be understood as a cultural feminist, a woman writer documenting problems of regional instability stemming from the clash between civil rights and feminist movements and the power struggles within an antiquated patriarchal social system, thereby exposing the insufficiency of male dominance and the sexual violence that occurs within such a system.

While feminist approaches do not necessarily preclude the theology generally associated with O'Connor's work, the increasing secularity of today's audience requires O'Connor scholars to broaden the scope of criticism. The "old" ways of looking at O'Connor's work are insufficient: she demands more from her readers. O'Connor's stories challenge us to look deeper, to re-read and re-adjust to new perspectives in an effort to construct our own strategies of resistance. Feminist readers should use O'Connor's difference to explore innovative approaches—new ideas valuable for the ways in which they turn patriarchal notions around and against themselves (see Hirschmann and DiStefano)—and to provide fresh frames of reference for reading O'Connor. Recent investigations into O'Connor's life reveal insights that go beyond her Catholicism, providing a sense of the whole personality. Jean Cash's biography, *Flannery O'Connor: A Life* (2002), indicates that O'Connor was neither misogynistic nor victimized by self-hatred. Rather, she was comfortable enough with herself to focus clearly on her surroundings, her family and the social world in which she lived—a world of manners and movements, of spirit and body, of desire and ridicule. Bringing O'Connor face-to-face with "the feminist business" provides the means for the imaginative critical reappraisal of her work that will keep Flannery O'Connor at the forefront of American literature.

WORKS CITED

Cash, Jean. *Flannery O'Connor: A Life.* Knoxville: U of Tennessee P, 2002.

Fetterley, Judith. *The Resisting Reader: A Feminist Approach to American Fiction.* Bloomington: Indiana UP, 1978.

Gentry, Marshall Bruce. *Flannery O'Connor's Religion of the Grotesque.* Jackson: UP of Mississippi, 1986.

Giannone, Richard. "Displacing Gender: Flannery O'Connor's View From the Woods." *Flannery O'Connor: New Perspectives.* Ed. Sura P. Rath and Mary Neff Shaw. Athens: U of Georgia P. 73–95.

Hirschmann, Nancy J., and Christine DiStefano. "Revision, Reconstruction, and the Challenge of the New." *Revisioning the Political: Feminist Reconstructions of Traditional Concepts in Western Political Theory.* Boulder: Westview P, 1996. 1–25.

Humm, Maggie. "Feminist Literary Theory." *Contemporary Feminist Theories.* Ed. Stevi Jackson and Jackie Jones. Washington Square: New York UP, 1998. 194–212.

Lamb, Sharon. Introduction. *New Versions of Victims: Feminists Struggle with the Concept.* New York: New York UP, 1999. 1–12.

O'Connor, Flannery. *Habit of Being.* Ed. Sally Fitzgerald. 1979. New York: Noonday-Farrar, 1988.

———. *Mystery and Manners.* Ed. Sally Fitzgerald and Robert Fitzgerald. 1969. New York: Noonday-Farrar, 1970.

Prown, Katherine Hemple. *Revising Flannery O'Connor: Southern Literary Culture and the Problem of Female Authorship.* Charlottesville: UP of Virginia, 2001.

Rath, Sura P. Introduction. *Flannery O'Connor: New Perspectives.* Ed. Sura P. Rath and Mary Neff Shaw. Athens: U of Georgia P, 1996. 1–11.

Reesman, Jeanne Campbell. "Women, Language and the Grotesque in Flannery O'Connor and Eudora Welty." In Rath and Shaw 38–56.

Retallack, Joan. ":Re:Thinking:Literary:Feminism: (three essays onto shaky grounds)." *Feminist Measures: Soundings in Poetry and Theory.* Ed. Lynn Keller and Cristanne Miller. Ann Arbor: U of Michigan P, 1994. 344–77.

Shands, Kerstin. *Embracing Space: Spatial Metaphors in Feminist Discourse.* Westport: Greenwood P, 1999.

Sorisio, Carolyn. "A Tale of Two Feminisms: Power and Victimization in Contemporary Feminist Debate." *Third Wave Agenda: Being Feminist, Doing Feminism.* Ed. Leslie Heywood and Jennifer Drake. Minneapolis: U of Minnesota P, 1997. 134–49.

Westling, Louise. "Flannery O'Connor's Mothers and Daughters." *Twentieth Century Literature: A Scholarly and Critical Journal* 24 (1978): 510–22.

O'Connor and *The Feminine Mystique*: "The Limitations That Reality Imposed"

ROBERT DONAHOO

> ...in the end, a woman, as a man, has the power to choose, and to make her own heaven or hell. —"Preface and Acknowledgements" in *The Feminine Mystique*

What's wrong with Flannery O'Connor's women?

There is little doubt that O'Connor's fiction displays a number of memorable female characters. From Leora Watts and Sabbath Lily Hawks in *Wise Blood* to The Grandmother in "A Good Man Is Hard to Find," Joy-Hulga in "Good Country People," and Ruby Turpin in "Revelation," O'Connor's fiction offers memorable female characters who are multi-dimensional, vital, and complexly meaningful. Yet since the 1980s, these women have tended to draw the ire of feminist critics, largely for their perceived failure to champion female empowerment and equality—charges that to many have seemed convincing. In her important study of 20th century Southern women authors, *Sacred Groves and Ravaged Gardens*, Louise Westling established much of the pattern of complaint. Damningly, Westling writes:

> Flannery O'Connor's vision could not countenance a feminine landscape controlled by the strong mother figures of the farm stories, for her world was ruled by a patriarchal authority which guarded His pastoral landscape as the Yahweh of the ancient Hebrews watched over Eden and the pastures of the Old Testament. (180)

For Westling, this situation requires a psychological explanation. Why would a Southern woman depict Southern women characters so negatively? Westling claims O'Connor "has inadvertently presented" "doubles of herself" that reveal "female self-loathing, powerlessness, and justified fear of masculine attack" (174).

Feminist critics who have examined O'Connor since Westling have often seen the same problems and offered similar explanations. Sarah Gordon's *Flannery O'Connor: The Obedient Imagination* approvingly cites Westling, refers to O'Connor's "attacks on female culture" (26), and claims, "*Obviously*, O'Connor did not embrace the matrilineal tradition, either in literature or in life; instead, she appears to have followed the route that Freud...describes as normative: that of embracing male tradition" (29, my emphasis). Even Katherine Hemple Prown's textual study of O'Connor's *Wise Blood* manuscripts wraps up its arguments with a psychological evaluation:

> Denying her female self, using male characters and masculinist narrative forms to express the limitations and constraints of female experience, O'Connor developed a complicated but unmistakably female aesthetic, one that grew out of her personal and professional situation. That she chose to reject feminism and instead bury her female self beneath layers of masculinist forms and conventions suggests that the aesthetic strategies adopted by women writers are not always overtly oppositional or subversive and may, on the contrary, involve a certain amount of self-hatred. (161)

Such speculation is not without value, but its insistence on finding an internal source for O'Connor's portraits of women may reveal as much the necessities imposed by theoretical commitments as it does about O'Connor's writing. Certainly, it discourages seeking out more tangible sources for these portraits, even though O'Connor herself described the work of the literary artist in terms of external observation and not internal exploration. In "The Nature and Aim of Fiction," O'Connor writes:

> Conrad said that his aim as a fiction writer was to render the highest possible justice to the visible universe. That sounds very grand, but it is really very humble. It means that he subjected himself at all time to the *limitations that reality imposed*, but that reality for him was not simply coextensive with the visible. He was interested in rendering justice to the visible universe because it suggested an invisible one. (*Mystery and Manners* 80, my emphasis)

This passage, with its accompanying quote from Conrad stressing the artist's "task" is "'by the power of the written word, to make you hear, to make you feel—it is, before all, to make you *see*'" (*Mystery and Manners* 80), has been frequently stressed in O'Connor criticism because it has allowed her work to be examined in terms of spiritual themes and ideas—making visible the suggested invisible. However, if one seeks sources or causes for O'Connor's women, it makes more sense to stress the idea of "the limitations that reality imposed." Such an emphasis prods the critical search to turn away from the question, "What shadowy theories of the mind and thought of Mary Flannery O'Connor do her writings reveal?" and toward this one: "What limited historical realities do O'Connor's works make clear that the artist O'Connor saw as material for her fiction?"

One answer to this question comes from an unlikely source: Betty Friedan's opening volley in the establishment of the modern American women's movement, *The Feminine Mystique*. The oddity of pairing Friedan and O'Connor is fairly obvious. Born in Peoria, Illinois, educated in an elite Eastern school, employed by a left-wing labor paper as a journalist until being fired for being pregnant with a second child, and then moving to the suburbs where she settled in as a housewife and mother of three (Halberstam 592–93), Friedan has come to be associated with causes such as abortion and lesbian rights which would seem to place an unbridgeable gap between her and O'Connor, the conservative southerner, educated in Georgia and Iowa, whose illness led her to live most of her adult life with her mother. But they share the Conradian drive "to see"—something Friedan, as she concludes *The Feminine Mystique*, places in each of the first two steps she encourages women to take:

> The first step...is *to see* housework for what it is—not a career, but something that must be done as quickly and efficiently as possible...The second step, and perhaps the most difficult for the products of sex-directed education, is *to see* marriage as it really is, brushing aside the veil of over-glorification imposed by the feminine mystique. (342, my emphasis)

Indeed, it could easily be argued that Friedan's book grew out of her seeing—her stunned response to questionnaires answered by the Smith College class of 1942 which Friedan planned to turn into an article for *McCall's* to be called "The Togetherness Woman" (Friedan, "Introduction to the Tenth Anniversary Edition" 7, Halberstam 595)—and is organized by seeing—its relentless presentation of personal statements and statistics to demonstrate "the desperation of so many American women" (26).

Moreover, O'Connor and Friedan were both looking at women over generally the same period: the 1950s and early 1960s, with O'Connor producing all of her major work between 1952 and her death in 1964, while Friedan's work on *The Feminine Mystique* began in 1957 and saw publication in 1963. Also, they focus their attention on the same kinds of women. O'Connor's major female characters are all white, frequently educated, and, if living mostly in the rural South, are not cut off from the larger world. Friedan's women, as Daniel Horowitz has pointed out, share many of these same privileges of race and class (208). And they are women of the same generation. Friedan was born in 1921, and O'Connor was born only four years later, with both women attending college during World War II—a fact that may account for their mutual fondness for imagery drawn from the recent Nazi concentration camps (See Horowitz 205 and Gentry 4–6). But the greatest point of interest lies in their actual presentation of women. For the images of American women in the 1950s and 60s that erupt from the pages of *The Feminine Mystique* are far from the flattering, healthy exemplars feminist critics have found so lacking in O'Connor. Indeed, by examining the images of women in Friedan's book and comparing them to women who populate O'Connor's work, the limited reality that O'Connor's view of art led her to use becomes strikingly clear.

At its core, Friedan's book is an examination of what she calls, "a problem of identity—a stunting or evasion of growth that is perpetuated by the feminine mystique" (77), and she makes clear that this stunting is the result of women being offered a choice of only two identities representing a false dichotomy: "In that corner, the fiery, man-eating feminist, the career woman—loveless, alone. In this corner, the gentle wife and mother—loved and protected by her husband, surrounded by her adoring children" (101). As part of her relentless attack on the second half of this choice, Friedan spends a considerable number of pages to show that, rather than aiding and helping her children, the home-centered mother was actually psychologically harming them. She notes, for instance, that many Freudian-based studies linked the "millions of American men…incapable of facing the shock of war" (189) with failed mothers and argued for a return to the home by women. However, she responds: "the mothers of the maladjusted soldiers, the insecure and impotent postwar males, were not independent educated career women, but self-sacrificing, dependent, martyred-housewife 'moms'" (190). For Friedan, the negative effect of these mothers results from what she terms a "destructive symbiosis" (190) that she sees as a predictable result of women being denied any outlet for their talents and energies beyond the home. Surprisingly, perhaps, Friedan has much more to say about the negative effects upon males raised by women committed to the feminine mystique than she does about negative effects upon females—a situation illustrated in her four-step schema by which she sees the feminine mystique perpetuating itself:

> 1. By permitting girls to evade tests of reality, and real commitments…by the promise of magical fulfillment through marriage, the feminine mystique arrests their development at an infantile level, short of personal identity, with an inevitably weak core of self.
> 2. The greater her own infantilism, and the weaker her core self, the earlier the girl will seek "fulfillment" as a wife and mother and the more exclusively she will live through her husband and children…
> 3. Since the human organism has an intrinsic urge to grow, a woman who evades her own growth by clinging to the childlike protection of the housewife role will…suffer increasingly severe pathology…Her motherhood will be increasingly pathological, both for her and for her children…Mothers with infantile selves will have even more infantile children, who will retreat even earlier into phantasy from the tests of reality.
> 4. The signs of this pathological retreat will be more apparent in boys, since even in childhood boys are expected to commit themselves to tests of reality which the feminine mystique permits the girls to evade in sexual phantasy. But these very expectations ultimately make the boys grow further toward a strong self and make the girls the worst victims, as well as the "typhoid Marys" of the progressive dehumanization of their own children. (290)

Whatever one feels about the sociological or psychological accuracy of Friedan's ideas, there is little doubt that they are mirrored in O'Connor's writing. Consider O'Connor's often anthologized story "Good Country People." Initially, Mrs. Hopewell may seem not to reflect Friedan's ideas since she has "divorced her husband long ago" (274) and runs her farm successfully on her own. However, the story makes clear that Mr. Freeman is the "farmer" (272) and that Mrs. Hopewell's life is limited to her home (she is most frequently depicted in housewife-like activities such as gardening and cooking) and to her daughter. Moreover, despite Joy-Hulga's striving for independence, her mother considers her "still a child" (277), and she worries that her daughter's educational advancement (her taking a PhD has "left Mrs. Hopewell at a complete loss") has unsuited her for the real life of wife and mother: "she didn't like dogs or cats or birds or flowers or nature or nice young men. She looked at nice young men as if she could smell their stupidity" (276). Most importantly, in providing her daughter a sanctuary from the life Joy-Hulga claims to desire (lecturing in a university), Mrs. Hopewell has, as Friedan would expect, prevented her daughter from facing the tests that might have prepared her to deal with Manley Pointer—a name whose phallic implications make clear that he represents some kind of sexual "phantasy." In short, Mrs. Hopewell's acceptance of a passive home-centered role plays a part in Joy-Hulga's victimization.

Friedan's picture of American mothers, however, goes even further. She cites at length therapists who have found a link between mothers who accept the roles required by the feminine mystique and the rise in juvenile delinquency. She writes:

> The symbiotic love or permissiveness which has been the translation of mother love during the years of the feminine mystique is not enough to create a social conscience and strength of character in a child. For this it takes a mature mother with a firm core of self, whose own sexual, instinctual needs are integrated with social conscience. "Firmness bespeaks a parent who has learned…how all of his major goals may be reached in some creative course of action." (297)

Again, O'Connor's writings reflect a similar observation. From the bratty June Star and John Wesley of "A Good Man Is Hard to Find" to the frighteningly cruel Scofield and Wesley of "Greenleaf" and the angry and violent Mary Grace of "Revelation," O'Connor's stories abound with children whose behavior is seen as or implies an absence of discipline. When Mary Grace responds rudely to Ruby Turpin, her mother acts in a way Friedan might find paradigmatic:

> "I think the worst thing in the world," she said, "is an ungrateful person. To have everything and not appreciate it. I know a girl," she said, "who has parents who would give her anything, a little brother who loves her dearly, who is getting a good education, who wears the best clothes, but who can never say a kind word to anyone, who never smiles, who just criticizes and complains all day long."

> "Is she too old to paddle?" Claud asked.
>
> The girl's face was almost purple.
>
> "Yes," the lady said, "I'm afraid there's nothing to do but leave her to her folly. Some day she'll wake up and it'll be too late." (499)

Swaddled in comfort and protected by her family, Mary Grace is incapable of reacting civilly to the middle-class pieties and self-satisfied assertions of Mrs. Turpin. The same attitudes that provoke laughter in readers and a satiric tone from the narrator drive Mary Grace to hurl a textbook at Ruby's head and an insult at her mind: "'Go back to hell where you came from, you old wart hog'" (500). If these actions lead to Ruby's revelation, they have less positive results for Mary Grace: she is pinned to the floor, injected with drugs, and carried off in an ambulance—presumably for treatment from the same type of therapists Friedan interviewed—while her mother can only sit on the floor and voice "tremulous moans" (501).

Readings such as this make one thing clear: whatever else we want to say about O'Connor's stories, the reality they depict is not inherently different from that documented and decried by arguably the most influential American feminist voice of the day. Furthermore, reading an anti-female bias into O'Connor's plots and characters overlooks the limitations imposed by the reality of the visible, historical universe her writings seek to render. Yet such historical neglect has not been uncommon. Cindy Beringer, for instance, in an insightful article that pointedly diagnoses the flaws of several of O'Connor's mothers, nevertheless interprets "Greenleaf" as seeking to "keep firmly in place" "the patriarchal social and economic system" (140). And rather than seeing Mrs. Greenleaf's violent death as the result of the very flaws her analysis reveals, Beringer concludes: "Having displaced a man at the head of the patriarchy, Mrs. May must be brought down and forced to face her weakness before men as well as before God" (140).

However politically correct or emotionally satisfying such conclusions are, they ignore the fact that Friedan's groundbreaking work to expand the roles available to women also forces women who have accepted the feminine mystique to face similar judgment. In fact, one particular comment by Friedan is highly appropriate for the very story that elicits Beringer's judgment. While focusing on the harmful effects of feminine mystique mothering, Friedan quotes with approval a therapist who reported treating a woman whose need for fulfillment through her child had left the child with "no sense of himself as a separate being at all" (296). Friedan writes:

> The strange thing was, the therapist said, like so many other women of this era of the "feminine role," in her endeavor to be a "real woman," a good wife and mother, "she was really playing a very masculine role...She was pushing everyone around—dominating the children's lives, ruling the house with an iron hand, managing the carpentry, nagging her husband to do odd jobs he never finished, managing the finances, supervising the recreation and the education—and her husband was just the man who paid the bills." (296–97)

In O'Connor's tale, the narrator reports that Mrs. May's

> city friends said she was the most remarkable woman they knew, to go, practically penniless and with no experience, out to a rundown farm and make a success of it. "Everything is against you," she would say, "the weather is against you and the dirt is against you and the help is against you. They're all in league against you. There's nothing for it but an iron hand!"
>
> "Look at Mamma's iron hand!" Scofield would yell and grab her arm and hold it up so that her delicate blue-veined little hand would dangle from her wrist like the head of a broken lily. The company always laughed. (321–22)

Though Friedan's passage does not seem to emphasize the irony that women who have submitted to the feminist mystique are becoming, as a consequence, masculinized, O'Connor's passage does, and the use by both writers of the image of the "iron hand" suggests that they find in this move an objectionable form of oppression or even a self-perpetuating cycle of abuse. Seen in this light, Mrs. May's violent death is not a punishment and blame, but an imaging of the invisible reality that she is already dead, impaled on the two prong-alternative of the feminine mystique. To borrow two other images from Friedan—both of which are highly appropriate to use in relation to O'Connor—Mrs. May's invisible reality is that she has "walked into" a "comfortable concentration camp" (308) or she is part of the "millions of American women" whom the feminine mystique "has succeeded in burying...alive" (336).

But it isn't merely O'Connor's mothers who seem to have their source in the lives of women described in *The Feminine Mystique*. For Friedan, the woman who seeks to find her identity through domination of her children's lives is the spawn of one of the mystique's core ideas: that women can and should be happy in the role of a housewife. Friedan writes:

> The feminine mystique says that the highest value and the only commitment for women is the fulfillment of their own femininity...The mistake, says the mystique, the root of women's troubles in the past is that women envied men, women tried to be like men, instead of accepting their own nature, which can find fulfillment only in sexual passivity, male domination, and nurturing maternal love.
>
> But the new image this mystique gives to American women is the old image: "Occupation: housewife." The new mystique makes the housewife-mothers, who never had a chance to be anything else, the model for all women...Beneath the sophisticated trappings, it simply makes certain concrete, finite, domestic aspects of feminine existence—as it was lived by women whose lives where confined, by necessity, to cooking, cleaning, washing, bearing children—into a religion, a pattern by which all women must now live or deny their femininity. (43)

The Feminine Mystique relentlessly attacks "Occupation: housewife" as a positive option for women. Through her language (notice as examples the words "trappings" and "confined" in the passage above) as well as her arguments, Friedan paints the image of the happy housewife as a "stunting or evasion of growth" (77) and a "lack of identity" (181) and, most tellingly, a form of culturally enforced mental retardation:

> Some decades ago, certain institutions concerned with the mentally retarded discovered that housework was peculiarly suited to the capacities of feeble-minded girls. In many towns [and this is certainly true of the Central Hospital for the Mentally Ill located in Milledgeville, O'Connor's home], inmates of institutions for the mentally retarded were in great demand as houseworkers, and housework was much more difficult then than it is now. (255)

Moreover, Friedan makes use of powerful anecdotes and devastating statistics to demonstrate the consequences of attempting to live such an image. At one point, she writes of an "upper-income" housing development in which the "mystique of feminine fulfillment [through mothering and housework] was...literally followed":

> ...what was mummy really like? Sixteen out of the twenty-eight [housewives interviewed] were in analysis or analytical psychotherapy. Eighteen were taking tranquilizers; several had tried suicide; and some had been hospitalized for varying periods, for depression or vaguely diagnosed psychotic states. ("You'd be surprised at the number of these happy suburban wives who simply go berserk one night, and run shrieking through the street without any clothes on," said the local doctor, not a psychiatrist, who had been called in, in such emergencies.) (235)

Surprisingly, perhaps, to those who see O'Connor so out of sympathy with feminist concerns, the happy housewife hardly receives gentler treatment in her fiction. Her most familiar happy housewife is the character referred to only as "the children's mother" in "A Good Man Is Hard to Find." Throughout the story, this woman's identity is submerged beneath that of her husband and children, beginning with her introduction in dehumanized terms: "a young woman in slacks, whose face was as broad and innocent as a cabbage and was tied around with a green head-kerchief that had two points on the top like a rabbit's ears. She was sitting on the sofa, feeding the baby his apricots out of a jar" (117). Unlike every other member of the household, she expresses no opinion about the family's vacation plans, and on the trip itself her only actions are to act as holder for the infant and to mechanically feed dimes into the nickelodeon at Red Sammy's (121). After the wreck, she does find a voice, though the text describes her speaking as "hoarsely" (125); and, despite having the most series injuries of anyone in the family—"she *only* had a cut down her face and a broken shoulder" (125, my emphasis)—she is largely ignored by her family and the text until, making "heaving noises as if she couldn't get her breath," she is led away to her execution and gives a final feminine, "Yes, thank you," to her killers (131).

The clear satire of such a look at the passive housewife of the 1950s is pushed even further in "The Life You Save May Be Your Own"—a story published in the same year as "A Good Man Is Hard to Find." Here, the happy housewife is literally a mentally challenged woman, the daughter Lucynell. Her mother portrays her virtues to Mr. Shiftlet in terms of her domestic work skills—"She can sweep the floor, cook, wash, feed the chickens, and hoe" (149)—and her passivity: "One that can't talk...can't sass you back or use foul language. That's the kind for you to have" (151). Moreover, the text asserts that she has no language except for what Mr. Shiftlet teaches her (150). To the "pale youth" in "The Hot Spot," she may look like "an angel of Gawd" (154), but to Mr. Shiftlet—her husband—she is a "hitchhiker" to be used in order to acquire a car, then abandoned (155). While it is certainly possible to see her in theological terms (See Ragen 104–5, for example), Lucynell also stands as a satiric portrait of a 1950s American wife.

More serious but just as devastating in its critique of the happy housewife is a story published a year later than "Good Man" and "Life You Save": "A Circle in the Fire." For Westling, this story is another example in O'Connor's writing of "masculine invasion" (167) and/or the "destruction of female control over the land" (166). However, the story looks rather different when recognizing Mrs. Cope as another version of the happy housewife, and she does fit the description. The story depicts her doing such housewifely tasks as weeding flowerbeds (175) and acting as hostess to the uninvited boys (181). Her self-worth clearly derives from her domestic work; she tells Mrs. Pritchard, "I have the best kept place in the county and do you know why? Because I work. I've had to work to save this place and work to keep it…I don't let anything get ahead of me and I'm not always looking for trouble. I take it as it comes" (178). Moreover, the nature of her "work" is called into question not only by the presence of Mrs. Pritchard as a hired hand but also by the text's insertion of African Americans who are shown doing the actual labor of the farm (176). And far from being happy in this situation, Mrs. Cope, despite her often repeated claim that "We have a lot to be thankful for" (177), is clearly frustrated. The text uses "muttered" (175), "shouted" (176), "sighed," "snapped" (177), "sharply" (178), "shriek" (181), "military" (188), and "scream" (193) as some of the descriptors of her utterances, and it bluntly states that, "Mrs. Cope was always afraid someone would get hurt on her place and sue her for everything she had" (180). Mrs. Cope even pronounces herself disappointed in her daughter: "'Why do you have to look like an idiot?' she asked. 'Suppose company were to come? When are you going to grow up? What's going to become of you? I look at you and I want to cry! Sometimes you look like you might belong to Mrs. Pritchard!'" (190). Seen as a whole, Mrs. Cope's image is hardly that of a contented, successful woman. Rather, she is better viewed as another assault on the happy housewife myth—an assault culminated by prophetic fire that burns away the masking material success of Mrs. Cope (and all such happy housewives) to reveal the barren life beneath it.

Seeing the happy housewife as a myth links directly to another image of women shared by Friedan and O'Connor: the frustration of the intelligent woman in a society that demands obeisance to the feminine mystique. Friedan refers directly to the "desperation" of American women (26) who in the 1950s found themselves asking, "What kind of woman was she if she did not feel this mysterious fulfillment waxing the kitchen floor?" (19). She also clearly defines the cause of such self-questioning as being forced to "deny their minds" and "deny the reality of a changing world" (66). To encourage such denial, Friedan sees 1950s American society persistently degrading education for women, offering as evidence such statements as Margaret Mead's claim that, "If women are to be restless and questing, even in the face of childbearing, they must be made so through education" (quoted 142) and Helene Deutsch's assertion, "Women's intellectuality is to a large extent paid for by the loss of valuable feminine qualities…All observations point to the fact that the intellectual woman is masculinized; in her warm, intuitive knowledge has yielded to cold, unproductive thinking" (quoted 173). For Friedan, such arguments pressure women to choose between the mystique's two false options, ignoring the actual results of education for women (175), and she notes that accepting the lonely feminist vs. beloved wife view of the world has had dire consequences for women:

> …by choosing femininity over the painful growth to full identity, by never achieving the hard core of self that comes not from fantasy but from mastering reality, these girls are doomed to suffer ultimately that bored, diffuse feeling of purposelessness, non-existence, non-involvement with the world that can be called *anomie*, or lack of identity, or merely felt as the problem that has no name. (181)

Such comments become particularly relevant for O'Connor when Friedan connects them to the women scholar. Friedan writes,

> the woman scholar was suspect, simply by virtue of being one. She was not just working to support her home; she must have been guilty of an unfeminine commitment to have kept working in her field all those hard, grinding, ill-paid years to the Ph.D. In self-defense, she sometimes adopted frilly blouses or another innocuous version of the feminine protest…M.D. or Ph.D., those hats and frilly blouses say, *let nobody question our femininity*. But the fact is, their femininity was questioned. (158)

It isn't hard to jump from this passage to Hulga Hopewell of "Good Country People," though the jump is not made without hazard. Clearly, Hulga, who is "highly educated" (271) and possesses a Ph.D., lives in a cloud of sexual suspicion—a questioning implied by Mrs. Freeman's flaunting of her daughter's bouts with morning sickness and raised directly by Hulga's mother, who, "could not help but feel that it would have been better if the child had not taken the Ph.D. It had certainly not brought her out any...She was brilliant but she didn't have a grain of sense" (276). On the other hand, Hulga can seem to be a woman unaffected by the pressure to deny her mind. She quotes the philosopher Malebranche to her mother, wears unstylish clothes (276), and achieves what she considers "one of her major triumphs" by defeating her mother's attempts "to turn her dust into Joy" and, instead, turning "herself into Hulga" (275). However, despite the desire of some critics to read Hulga as a victim of O'Connor's desire to quash any attempts at liberation, she is more accurately understood as a victim, not of authorial anti-feminism, but of historical gender reality. For like many of the educated women whom Friedan cites, Hulga never puts her education to use. Convinced by doctors that she is physically incapable of a career, Hulga has settled into a "joy-less" existence away from the urban world (276). If, as another historical critic has suggested, this situation parallels that of American intellectuals in the 1950s (Bacon 46), it even more closely suggests the situation, as Friedan paints it, of American women in that era. Moreover, when the phallically named Manley Pointer appears, Hulga rushes toward the traditionally feminine, dreaming of sex and even daintily scenting herself with "some Vapex on the collar" (284).

The reality is that Hulga has never escaped the choice Friedan claims confronted American women in the 1950s. Rather, she has elected the option of "the career woman—loveless, alone" (101), still accepting the feminine mystique's understanding of the world. Significantly, Friedan argues that this understanding has its basis in Freudian psychology, which, she claims, sees women's problems in terms of deficiencies categorized as "penis envy" (117–18). And, of course, O'Connor's text depicts Hulga as suffering a lack—created in a hunting (a stereotypically male sport) accident—that she has dealt with by attaching a phallic object to her body. Put another way, Hulga has accepted the feminine mystique's definition of her position and attempted to deal with it by pursuing the masculinizing option. However, if there is one thing that the text and countless critical commentaries on this story make clear, the text does not see Hulga's problem as her missing leg/penis. Rather, as O'Connor herself once commented, "there is a wooden part of her soul that corresponds to her wooden leg" (*Mystery and Manners* 99). In taking the leg, symbolically castrating her, the living penis in the story functions just as Friedan sees the feminine mystique functioning: taking away the only alternative it ever offered to being anything other than "the gentle wife and mother—loved and protected by her husband" (101).

Should we read this act as Westling and other feminists have encouraged us to do, as the author's implied rejection of the possibility of female development? I don't think so. After all, "Good Country People" ends with a powerful contrast. Hulga's face is described as "churning" and turned toward an "opening" through which she sees a transformed landscape while Mrs. Freeman and Mrs. Hopewell statically dig up onions and proclaim their own certainty (291). The imagery suggests Hulga has begun the process of development and growth that Friedan claims is the true alternative to accepting the feminine mystique. And if O'Connor offers only a vague vision of the outcome of Hulga's experience, Friedan also in 1963 hadn't formed a clear picture of what lay ahead for American women. Her final paragraph begins with a series of questions, the first of which is, "Who knows what women can be when they are finally free to become themselves?" (378). O'Connor's texts never claim such knowledge, for, as Frederick Crews has observed, "O'Connor's works...are not finally about salvation but about doom—the sudden and irremediable realization that there is no exit from being, for better or worse, exactly who one is" (165). Reading O'Connor in conjunction with Friedan makes a strong case that the doom is historically, not authorially, imposed.

Even in *Wise Blood*, O'Connor's first novel and one that limits female characters to supporting roles, the depiction of women is far more suggestive of the problems Friedan would call the feminine mystique than they are of psychological imbalance. For Friedan, one of the markers of women's harassment by the feminine mystique is a distorted view of sexuality. In a chapter entitled, "The Sex-Seekers," Friedan documents through popular movies, novels, psychological commentary, and personal interviews a tendency of American women to turn to sex in order, as one woman says, "'to feel alive'" (258). Friedan writes, "For the woman who lives according to the feminine mystique, there is no road to achievement, or status, or identity, except the sexual one: the achievement of sexual conquest, status as a desirable sex object, identity as a sexually successful wife and mother"

(266). Again, "They [young girls] use sex…to erase their lack of identity; it seldom matters who the boy is; the girl almost literally does not 'see' him when she has as yet no sense of herself. Nor will she ever have a sense of herself if she uses the easy rationalizations of the feminine mystique to evade in sex-seeking the efforts that lead to identity" (277). Moreover, Friedan links this seeking by women for identity and fulfillment in sex to male hostility—even male homosexuality (271–76). She also notes its lack of success for women: "Instead of fulfilling the promise of infinite orgastic bliss, sex in the America of the feminine mystique is becoming a strangely joyless national compulsion, if not a contemptuous mockery…Sex has become depersonalized, seen in terms of…exaggerated symbols" (261).

Though *Wise Blood* is not one of the novels Friedan cites as reflecting this situation, both Leora Watts and Sabbath Lily Hawkes fit comfortably into Friedan's paradigm, though one would never guess such a thing from critics such as Gordon and Prown, both of whom see these women, in Gordon's words, as "obstacle[s] in the male's spiritual quest" (98; see also Prown 116). Such views, however, are themselves a submission to Hazel Motes' warped perception. Certainly, Haze views them as steps in his rejection of God, telling Mrs. Watts, "What I mean to have you know is: I'm no goddam preacher" (34), and feeling, in relation to Sabbath, that, "he should have a woman, not for the sake of the pleasure in her, but to prove that he didn't believe in sin since he practiced what was called it" (110). But these women have an existence beyond Haze's view of them, as the text's denial to Haze of narrative control implies, and that existence is in line with Friedan's picture of victims of the feminine mystique.

Mrs. Watts is connected to Friedan's ideas in several ways, beginning with the novel's insistence of seeing her as a collection of body parts: a large white knee seen through a "convenient crack" in a window shade (32), "very yellow hair and white skin that glistened with a greasy preparation" (33), toenails being cut, a pink tipped tongue, and teeth "small and pointed and speckled with green" (33–34). There is little erotic or tantalizing about her or her attitude toward sex. Indeed, as what could be termed a "professional sex seeker," Mrs. Watts is merely punching the clock with Haze, bored with her existence as the perversely Joycean image of her cutting her toenails suggests. Moreover, she finds little pleasure in her sexual acts with Haze, as Haze himself remembers: "he had not been very successful with Mrs. Watts. When he finished, he was like something washed ashore on her, and she had made obscene comments about him…He didn't know what she would say when he opened the door and she saw him there" (59). Indeed, one of the last images the novel supplies of her is very much in line with Friedan's sense of sex having become "strangely joyless," a "compulsion," a "mockery," "depersonalized" (261). The novel reads, "It was plain that she was so well-adjusted that she didn't have to think anymore" (60). Clearly, readers are meant to see a woman who is unfulfilled by sex and who, by accepting expressions of sexuality as her only means of being, leads an unfulfilled, pathetic existence.

Sabbath Lily Hawkes makes even more strongly the case for seeing *Wise Blood*'s women as victims of the feminine mystique rather than victims of the author's misogyny. Seen only from Haze's perspective, she might well be merely a homely girl he can use to make his theological points, but O'Connor's text—not just the manuscripts but the published novel—supply two scenes where the reader can see Sabbath without Haze filtering the view. In a brief scene involving only Sabbath and her father, Sabbath shows she is less interested in Haze as an individual than as a means of finding and defining her life:

> "Listen here," she said, sitting down on the cot with [Asa Hawkes], "you help me to get him and then you go away and do what you please and I can live with him."
>
> "He don't even know you exist," Hawkes said.
>
> "Even if he don't," she said, "that's all right. That's howcome I can get him easy. I want him and you ought to help and then you could go on off like you want to." (109)

As Friedan might note, Sabbath makes no mention of establishing a life apart from her father via a career or education. For her, the only avenue away from dear old dad is a man.

A chapter later, when Sabbath surprises Haze in his car, she tells him of two letters she has written to a newspaper advice columnist, asking, "Dear Mary, I am a bastard and a bastard shall not enter the kingdom of heaven as we all know, but I have this personality that makes boys follow me. Do you think I should neck or not?" (119). When the columnist responded with encouragement that Sabbath should not let religion "warf" her (119), Sabbath tells Haze she wrote a second letter to make her intentions clear: "Dear Mary, What I really want to know is should I go the whole hog or not? That's my real problem" (119–20). This correspondence makes clear that for

Sabbath sex is being well-adjusted—not sex with a particular person but with boys in general. Not surprisingly, then, she quickly becomes the sexual aggressor in her relationship to Haze, sneaking to his bed at night (146 and 168), attaching herself to him so tightly that Haze is driven to try sneaking away (185–86). Even more clearly, the closing images of Sabbath as mother to the "new jesus" establishes that she is using sex to give her life some fulfillment. She tells the mummy, "Call me Momma now" and then, referring to Haze, says to the mummy, "Ask your daddy yonder where he was running off to" (187). Even when Haze destroys their mummy/child and Sabbath tells him, "I knew when I first seen you you were mean and evil," she refuses to release her grip on Haze, and the chapter ends with Haze declaring his intention to sleep and Sabbath responding, "You ain't going to get none" (189).

Such scenes illustrate what *The Feminine Mystique* calls "playing house at nineteen" to evade "the responsibility of growing up" (281). Moreover, Haze's hostility echoes Friedan's ideas about the response of a young man to a girl's dependence on him "even as he helplessly succumbs to the sexual invitation" (280). In short, rather than misogynistic portrayals, both Mrs. Watts and Sabbath Hawkes, in light of Friedan's book, stand as psychologically real portrayals of women in this time period—women who use sex to seek to establish some kind of identity.

A similar observation is possible about *Wise Blood*'s other two major female figures: Haze's mother and Mrs. Flood—both mother figures, though of different types. Haze's biological mother is fierce and chastising as he remembers her beating him across the legs with a stick after he has seen the naked woman at the carnival (63). Moreover, acting like a wounded conscience, a vision of her is resurrected when, near the end of the novel, Haze puts on her glasses (187). While Sarah Gordon suggests we should see Haze's mother as a rare image of a powerful female legacy that Haze must overcome (117), in light of Friedan's *Feminine Mystique* it makes at least equal sense to see her as the "man-eating mother" who, limited by the feminine mystique from expressing herself in any way except through her family and children, becomes "parasitic" and "keep[s]...husbands and sons from growing up" (274). In other words, she is not a result of O'Connor's limited gender views but an observed reality of the 1950s.

This idea is supported by O'Connor's use of Mrs. Flood for the controlling perspective of *Wise Blood*'s closing chapter. Almost from her first appearance in the novel, Mrs. Flood is pictured as someone who keeps house for others: cleaning and providing meals for a fee. When the final chapter begins, instead of modifying this motherly picture, the text accentuates it as Mrs. Flood gives Haze advice about Sabbath (216) and worries over his eating habits (217–18). Even when she considers marrying him, Mrs. Flood thinks in terms of money and security, not sex (219), and she finally decides merely to "keep him" (225). When the police return Haze's dying body to her, the emphasis is placed again on her desire to mother him: "I've been waiting for you," she says. "And you needn't to pay any more rent but have it free here, any way you like, upstairs or down. Just however you want it and with me to wait on you, or if you want to go on somewhere, we'll both go" (231). Clearly, the text wants us to see Mrs. Flood making her self-hood reliant on Haze. In short, we see her, even if only briefly, surrender completely the ideals of the feminine mystique, becoming, in Friedan's words, a woman "who has no goal, no purpose, no ambition patterning her days into the future, making her stretch and grow"—a woman who "is committing a kind of suicide" (336).

If such an image seems to reinforce the idea that this novel offers only negative views of women, it should be remembered that not only is the novel merely observing that such a pattern is one Mrs. Flood elects for herself, but it also points to attempts to disrupt her decision. The novel does not allow Haze to accept or encourage her decision. Instead, by depicting Haze as "moving farther and farther away, farther and farther into the darkness" (232), the novel refuses to project any positive outcome to Mrs. Flood's decision. In short, it not only fails to encourage the feminine mystique, but, like Friedan's book, it attempts to unmask it.

I would argue that such an attempt to unmask the feminine mystique trapping women of the 1950s is not an unconscious side effect of O'Connor's misogyny. Rather, it lies at the core of her role as a satirist—one who seeks to encourage change. Certainly, O'Connor herself does not seem to have accepted the plight of American women in the 1950s as unalterable. In a 1955 letter to Betty Hester, she writes, "If I were to live long enough and develop as an artist to the proper extent, I would like to write a comic novel about a woman—and what is more comic and terrible than the angular intellectual proud woman approaching God inch by inch with ground teeth" (*Habit of Being* 105–6). I would argue that the comic and terrible women of *Wise Blood* and the numerous stories discussed here should be seen as early manifestations of that never written novel. Moreover, linking O'Connor's fiction to Friedan's social manifesto confirms Patricia Yaeger's observation that O'Connor's women represent, "a particular remedy for cultural blockage" through the recovery of "an incredible fount of life-saving, script-saving anger" (113).

Questions, of course, remain—particularly the issue of Friedan's own historical accuracy (see Chafe 227–29 and Horowitz 210–13). If, as Chafe and Horowitz suggest, Friedan skewed her observations to make a more palatable and powerful book, why does O'Connor, whose personal library (see Kinney), letters and essays show no mention of Friedan, skew her observations along the same lines? In other words, work remains to delineate the lives of the real women who surrounded O'Connor. Nevertheless, the common view of women's conditions shared by O'Connor's fiction and *The Feminine Mystique* serves to undermine attempts to label O'Connor anti-feminist or to view her fiction outside its historical context. Indeed, within that context, O'Connor's work should be seen as sharing Friedan's desire to enable women to move beyond the feminine mystique, "break[ing] out of their comfortable concentration camps" and "fulfilling their own unique possibilities as separate human beings" (337)—something Friedan believed seeing the feminine mystique would set in motion. Undoubtedly, the two women would describe "unique possibilities" in different ways, but that doesn't negate the fact that the problem with O'Connor's women is the one Friedan describes: confinement within cultural definitions of "woman."

WORKS CITED

Bacon, Jon Lance. *Flannery O'Connor and Cold War Culture*. Cambridge: Cambridge UP, 1993.

Beringer, Cindy. "'I Have Not Wallowed': Flannery O'Connor's Working Mothers." *Southern Mothers: Fact and Fictions in Southern Women's Writing*. Ed. Nagueyalti Warren and Sally Wolff. Baton Rouge: Louisiana State UP, 1999. 124–41.

Chafe, William H. *The American Woman: Her Changing Social, Economic, and Political Roles, 1920–1970*. Oxford: Oxford UP, 1972.

Crews, Frederick. *The Critics Bear It Away: American Fiction and the Academy*. New York: Random House, 1992.

Friedan, Betty. *The Feminine Mystique*. 1963. New York: Laurel, 1983.

———. "Introduction to the Tenth Anniversary Edition." *The Feminine Mystique*. New York: Laurel, 1983.

Gentry, Bruce Marshall. *Flannery O'Connor's Religion of the Grotesque*. Jackson: UP of Mississippi, 1986.

Gordon, Sarah. *Flannery O'Connor: the Obedient Imagination*. Athens: U of Georgia P, 2000.

Halberstam, David. *The Fifties*. New York: Villard, 1993.

Horowitz, Daniel. *Betty Friedan and the Making of* The Feminine Mystique*: The American Left, the Cold War, and Modern Feminism*. Amherst: U of Massachusetts P, 1998.

Kinney, Arthur F. *Flannery O'Connor's Library: Resources of Being*. Athens: U of Georgia P, 1985.

O'Connor, Flannery. *The Complete Stories*. New York: Farrar, Straus and Giroux, 1971.

———. *The Habit of Being*. Ed. Sally Fitzgerald. New York: Farrar, Straus, and Giroux, 1979.

———. *Mystery and Manners*. Ed. Sally Fitzgerald and Robert Fitzgerald. New York: Farrar, Straus and Giroux, 1969.

———. *Wise Blood*. 2nd ed. New York: Farrar, Straus, and Giroux, 1952.

Prown, Katherine Hemple. *Revising Flannery O'Connor: Southern Literary Culture and the Problem of Female Authorship*. Charlottesville: UP of Virginia, 2001.

Ragen, Brian Abel. *A Wreck on the Road to Damascus*. Chicago: Loyola UP, 1989.

Westling, Louise. *Sacred Groves and Ravaged Gardens: The Fiction of Eudora Welty, Carson McCullers, and Flannery O'Connor*. Athens: U of Georgia P, 1985.

Yaeger, Patricia Smith. "The Woman without Any Bones: Anti-Angel Aggression in *Wise Blood*. *New Essays on Wise Blood*. Ed. Michael Kreyling. Cambridge: Cambridge UP, 1995. 91–116.

Flannery O'Connor's Struggle with Patriarchal Culture

VIRGINIA WRAY

Flannery O'Connor's reluctance to talk about her own personal and emotional life is well known. Although she could freely and quite generously converse about personal matters in the lives of many of her friends—Robert Lowell's breakdowns, Cecil Dawkins' loss of faith, Betty Hester's conversion, Maryat Lee's health, for example—she chose only rarely in her letters to initiate discussion of her own private life; she even frequently appeared to avoid such discussion when her correspondents apparently invited it. Only such close friends as Betty Hester and Maryat Lee successfully pushed her to risk occasional personal revelations. In a letter of 28 June 1956 to Betty Hester, shortly after Hester's first visit to Milledgeville, O'Connor wrote unguardedly about her family's "flat" demeanor: "I come from a family where the only emotion respectable to show is irritation. In some this tendency produces hives, in others literature, in me both" (997–98).

This rare glimpse of life in the O'Connor/Cline household well illustrates the "restraint" and "limitations" that Sarah Gordon argues characterize the effects of Southern patriarchal culture on women. Irritation in the Green Street house, no doubt, was restricted to the confines of the home, and O'Connor need not report in this letter to a female Georgian of her own generation that all the proprieties and niceties of Southern ladyhood, empty and hypocritical though they might well be, were required in public. What is most interesting about this glimpse into O'Connor's family life is not what it shows about the tenor of life with the O'Connors and the Clines, but rather the effects O'Connor declares that these restrictions and limitations had on her. Although typically humorous and seemingly exaggerated, her terse discussion of these effects is quite serious and perceptive: like the eruptions of hives, she claims her writing is a reaction to the constraints and limitations imposed upon her. Clearly, some of her very early unpublished writing is an overt, quite conscious rebellion against the Southern patriarchy that dictated these constraints and limitations; as O'Connor matures as a writer and joins the predominately male literary establishment, this rebellion submerges, becoming vested in several female children, finally reemerging openly in the character of Mary Grace in the very late story "Revelation."

Two pieces that O'Connor wrote for English 324 in the spring of 1943 at Georgia College evidence spirited attacks on some of the precepts of Southern ladyhood. The first piece, "Nine Out of Every Ten," signed with the clearly female pseudonym "Jane Shoebanks" (Driggers 2, File 4b) describes a young woman audaciously—and quite pleasurably—chewing a wad of gum. She fondles the gum with her tongue, moving it from side to side in her mouth and sliding it sensuously over the roof of her mouth. Just as she begins to blow a bubble, an older woman appears who, with her physical demeanor and her hasty departure from the girl, casts a clear and forceful judgment on the girl's unladylike behavior. The final sentence of the exercise shows the girl's—and possibly O'Connor's—ambivalent attitude when caught in such improper behavior: while she is described as moving casually on, her chewing keeping time to a popular waltz, her facial expression is pained by having been caught in her indecorous behavior.

The second piece, "The Cynosure," written for the same Georgia College class, is also attributed to a female pseudonym, "Gertrude Beachlock" (Driggers 2, File 4c). This description exercise, dated three weeks after "Nine Out of Every Ten," might well be a satire of the proper old woman in the gum-chewing piece. One Mrs. Peterson arrives half an hour early to a play, just as the theatre is opening. Obsessed with punctuality, she is equally obsessed with habit, demanding her usual seat by section, number, and row. This timely old creature of habit arrogantly orders the entire entourage of ushers to escort her to her seat and then, with reading glasses in place, inspects the program to her satisfaction before placing it in her purse and folding her hands in a ladylike pose to wait for the curtain. Clearly a parody of the cultured Southern lady, Mrs. Peterson is the target of the narrator's bile. Not only is she offensively rigid and demanding, but she also seems blind to the physical attractiveness of the ushers, an attractiveness mentioned by the narrator not once, but twice.

A two-page fragment of an untitled short story that Stephen Driggers places among the early Iowa manuscripts (4, File 9c) more strongly evidences young O'Connor's ability to rebel opening in her very early fiction against the expectations of Southern patriarchy on females. The protagonist Mary Flemming clearly has autobiographical overtones. She has named pet hens and a rooster for a cousin and two aunts who live next door, and when seen kissing the fowl by one Nora Pitts who stares from a window in a nearby apartment, Mary Flemming launches into a diversionary tactic designed to make Miss Pitts think she is crazy, an acceptable posture in the best of Southern culture. She first picks up and kisses a chicken again before throwing it back into the coal bin where it had been roosting. Then she picks up and kisses the rooster again before turning him upside down and thrusting her own neck forward and backward in imitation of the fowl. Her antics effect Miss Pitt's departure from the window, inviting Mary Flemming's return into the house after one last staged lunacy of blowing into the rooster's face.

Life inside the house with her mother explains Mary Flemming's need for camaraderie with the chickens: her mother barks a barrage of commands dictating proper appearance and behavior: hand washing, proper posture, held-in-stomach, table setting. Mary Flemming is subject even to physical makeover to help her conform to the prescribed attractive lady-like appearance: she wears braces on her teeth,[1] which she, of course, has neglected to put the rubber bands on, and corrective shoes, whose effects are minimized by her forgetting to walk on the outside of her feet and her failure to do her toe exercises at night. Her world, appropriately shown to us here in the common kitchen domain of women, is torturously constricted. Not surprisingly, then, when Mary Flemming disappears to the bathroom to install her rubber bands before her mother discovers her negligence, she tries another strategy to help her through her lot, but this time not feigned lunacy: she puts her face close to her reflection in the mirror and utters a male name, no doubt imagining the freedom she could have had she been born male.

Katherine Hemple Prown's book, *Revising Flannery O'Connor: Southern Literary Culture and the Problem of Female Authorship*, offers excellent analysis of the formative effect that O'Connor's study at the Iowa Writers' Workshop had on gender in her fiction. Taught exclusively by men and seeking access into the literary establishment largely controlled by men, O'Connor assumed a more masculine narrative voice. Her personal choice of dropping "Mary" from her name early in her Iowa days both defies the southern tradition of double female names and establishes a nominal androgynous identity in the world of letters akin to the male pseudonyms of numerous nineteenth-century female writers. With that new public identity and the masculinizing of her narrative voice came neophytehood in the male-dominated literary scene of the Writers' Workshop and, soon, in the national literary scene. With it also came O'Connor's relinquishing of blatant criticism and satire of patriarchal treatment of women present in some of the juvenilia. Nonetheless, criticism of patriarchy—both Southern and Catholic—occurs in the mature work, much more subtly, but still in the guise of rebellious children. Two stories from *A Good Man Is Hard to Find*, "A Temple of the Holy Ghost" and "A Circle in the Fire," both have near pubescent girls as protagonists who threaten violation of the Southern sexual taboos until patriarchal forces bring them back in line. Both girls are ultimately made compliant with patriarchal values, but in their initial rebellious spirit, they recall Mary Flemming from the Iowa fragment and the other defiant young girls in the juvenilia.

In "The Temple of the Holy Ghost" the unnamed twelve-year-old child, who, like Mary Flemming, wears braces (198), subverts her own blossoming curiosities about sex by mocking the blatant curiosities of her visiting older cousins from the convent school, Joanne and Susan. Aligned with the child's point of view, the narrator tells us that "neither of [the cousins] was bright" and had they not been sent to the convent school, "they wouldn't have done anything but think about boys" (197). According to the girls' mother, the convent school "would keep a grip on [the girls'] necks" (197). Indeed, the Catholic patriarchy thoroughly understands the depth and power of young girls' sexual curiosities and drives, and charges the sisters at the convent school with controlling the girls and acculturating them to the sexual mores of the Church. The story's title illustrates such instruction, comic though that instruction is as the girls recount it through teenage giggles: "Sister Perpetua said they were to say, 'Stop sir! I am a Temple of the Holy Ghost!' and that would put an end to it" (199). The mockery that the child makes of her cousins and their boy craziness to some degree appears unconscious self-admonishment. She is more sexually adroit and curious than she first appears. Her repeatedly expressed repulsion from Alonzo Myers' physical person, her suggestion of the Wilkins brothers as dates for the girls, and her fallacious description of the boys to her cousins suggest an awareness of physicality and pop sexual culture beyond her years. Her exaggeration of the boys' heights and her lies about their attire and car complete with "squirrel tail" (200) are not the fabrications of a child ignorant of the chemistry of physical attractions. Furthermore, her explanation of a rabbit's having had young by spitting them out of her mouth, though comic and desperate, ventures more of an anatomical understanding than do her fourteen-year-old cousins' inarticulate giggles.

What distinguishes the child from the boy crazy cousins is her sublimation of her nascent sexual feelings. Not only will she not sit with the four adolescents at dinner under the Japanese lanterns, but she also fantasizes herself a male to avoid her feelings, again recalling Mary Flemming and her vision of herself as male to avoid her mother's constant picking at her. The child in "The Temple of the Holy Ghost" imagines herself having fought in WW II, and when she speculates her future occupation, she begins with the traditionally masculine doctor and engineer and moves to saint and martyr, but interestingly never grants gender to either saint or martyr through any specific allusion. When she fantasizes such pranks as putting "a chicken carcass or a piece of beef liver" (204–5) in Joanne's and Susan's bed, she seems further to separate herself from her cousins by choosing a very boy-like prank predicated on disgust of girlish squeamishness. We truly see into the child through her fascination with any secondhand information she can glean about the hermaphrodite. Unable to comprehend two different sets of genitalia with only a single head, the narrator, in the guise of the child, imagines a church setting to replace the carnival setting, connecting the sanctity of the human body inherent in the biblical phrase "temple of the holy ghost" with the freak reportedly having insisted repeatedly that God had made him/her that way.

O'Connor is, of course, as she explained to Betty Hester in a 16 December 1955 letter, writing a story about purity, "an acceptance of what God wills for us" (976). The ending of the story, however, hints at a richer and not, I think, necessarily contradictory reading of this conventional and authorially conscious theological reading. During the benediction, the child's demeanor changes. "Her mind began to get quiet and then empty" (208), and as the priest raises the Host, she recalls the hermaphrodite and the freak's insistence of God's hand in creating his sexuality and his own acceptance of that sexuality. The child associates herself with the freak, and her calmed demeanor suggests her similar acceptance of self. The paragraph that follows, however, offers a striking and painful image of what may be the cost of this calm. As the child leaves the convent, "The big nun swooped down on her mischievously and nearly smothered her in the black habit, mashing the side of her face into the crucifix hitched onto her belt" (209). The predatory swooping action, the near smothering, the mashing of the crucifix into the child's face are all very unappealing images recalling the earlier claim that the sisters would control Joanne's and Susan's sexuality by keeping "a grip on their necks." The child's newfound calm with her own adolescent freakishness may be her simply having fallen into the Church's patriarchal constraints on sexuality, availing her a way to deal with her new feelings that is safe, but evasive.

O'Connor need not have intended any criticism of the Church's sexual education of young girls. But these images are there and speak loudly for themselves. Steeped in New Criticism as she was, she would, no doubt, press us to trust the tale, not the teller. She says as much to Betty Hester in a letter of 17 November 1956:

> You are right of course about not understanding the ordinary emotions any better than the extraordinary ones. But the writer doesn't have to understand, only reproduce...I certainly have no idea how I have written about some of the things I have, as they are things I am not conscious of having thought about one way or the other. Experiences must have some parallel relationship. (1007)

"A Circle in the Fire" presents another Mary Flemming-like twelve-year-old female protagonist with a mouthful of braces and the spunk to attempt to take on the patriarchy that threatens her and her mother. That threat manifests itself in the form of three adolescent boys with a look of "hardened hunger" (242), but no appetite for food, come against all prohibitions to mount and ride Mrs. Cope's horses. Much of the boys' invasion of the Cope farm is seen from Sally Virginia's point of view, often as she kneels at the window of her upstairs bedroom silently observing the skirmishes between the boys and her mother. As potentially funny as the child's kneeling tower-like observation of the brewing conflict below her may be, O'Connor never satirizes Sally Virginia's perspective, giving it great credence and inviting the reader to take her final actions when she descends the bedroom very seriously.

What Sally Virginia sees from her periphery perch is her single-parent mother who has always worked, doing a man's job of running the farm, rendered totally inept by three teenage boys. With no deference to age and living the patriarchal privileges of males, the boys simply overwhelm Mrs.

Cope. As Mrs. Pritchard says to Mrs. Cope multiple times about the boys' taking over of the farm, "There ain't a thing you can do about it" (243). Mrs. Cope's failed efforts to regain control play into the very patriarchy that gives the boys their power: she appeals to their gentlemanliness (242) casting herself, and by extension her daughter, in the role of lady. But the boys know their own power, know that acting like gentlemen would be by choice, not by necessity. They openly express disdain for women and have no intent of choosing deferential behavior toward what they have been taught to perceive as the weaker sex. When they sight Sally Virginia up in her window, the large boy speaks for the trio: "'Jesus,' he growled, 'another woman'" (242). Hearing the comment, the child is shaken to the bone. "She dropped back from the window and stood with her back against the wall, squinting fiercely as if she had been slapped in the face and couldn't see who had done it" (242).

Sally Virginia's foray into the woods the next morning is her "stalking out [of the] enemy" (248), using a strategy radically different from her mother's lady-like efforts to rid the farm of the boys. Prepubescent Sally Virginia sets out to fight fire with fire, donning a "pair of overalls over her dress...pull[ing] a man's old felt hat down as far as it would go on her head and...arming herself with two pistols in a decorated holster that she had fastened around her waist" (247). Mrs. Cope's "tragic look" when she sees Sally Virginia's get-up reflects the agony of a failed traditional Southern mother; her asking the girl when she was "going to grow up" is a mother's plea for a daughter's compliance with the values of the patriarchy, compliance the mother herself had long since given (247–48).

What happens in the woods when Sally Virginia finds the boys racing naked about a trough succeeds in instructing the young girl where her mother has failed. Ben Griffith saw the near explosive sexual power of this scene and helped O'Connor understand what she had written. In a 25 November 1955 letter to Betty Hester, O'Connor recounts Griffith's perceptions:

> He remarked that in these stories there was usually a strong kind of sex potential that was always turned aside and that this gave the stories some of their tension—as for instance in A Circle in the Fire [sic] where there is a strong possibility that the child in the woods with the boys may be attacked—but the attack takes another form. I really hadn't thought of it until he pointed it out but I believe it is a very perceptive comment. (971–72)

In an 8 December 1955 letter to Hester, O'Connor continues the discussion, defining graphically what she understands as the "sexual potential" Griffith had seen and that Hester appears to have romanticized in her previous letter to O'Connor:

> …on the matter of the possible attack on the child in A Circle in the Fire [sic], I think you are off because you assume I think that would be an act of passion, that the boys, if they attacked her, would be sharp enough to know that it would be their best revenge on Mrs. Cope; they would do it to humiliate the child and the mother, not to enjoy themselves. And children, particularly in numbers, are quite capable of using themselves in this way, of committing the most monstrous crimes out of the urge to destroy and humiliate. They might well have done this if they had seen the child behind the tree. I didn't let them see the child behind the tree. I couldn't have gone through that myself. (973)

O'Connor is certainly right to argue the potential meanness of the three boys and to see their motivation, should they attack the child, as intent to humiliate. What she doesn't see, or at least fails to express in this letter, is that the particulars of the potential meanness of the scene are not generic to children, but rather specific to males in a patriarchal culture. The boys have let the bull out on Mrs. Cope's farm, and he roams freely just as they in their primeval frolicking celebrate their own dominance of the farm and the women on it. Were these adolescent boys to see and rape the child, they would do it because they can do it, and because they feel an obligation to their patriarchal culture to strip her of her feigned masculine garb and fake penises, and force her back to the subservient role they believe essential to females.

The child's first and obvious fear is the sexual threat that dominates the scene. When she sees the boys naked, she hides behind a pine tree, "the side of her face pressed into the bark" (249). As O'Connor diverts the boys' potential meanness from rape to arson, Sally Virginia's more general fear comes into focus: her embrace of the tree suggests her desperate desire to return to the safety of her mother and the sanctuary her mother provides in her woods, a sanctuary the boys have come to destroy. Stripped of her feigned masculine power, her naive intent to take the boys on their terms more than failed, Sally Virginia intuits the wisdom of her mother's instruction: a southern woman cannot take the patriarchy on and win; she must capitulate to its power in order to then discover what integrity she can create for herself within her subservient place. "[W]eighted down with some new unplaced misery that she had never felt before," Sally Virginia is momentarily paralyzed (250). Finally, with "the imprint of the bark embossed red and white on the side of her face," Sally Virginia rushes back to the side of her mother, "star[ing] up at her face as if she had never seen it before" (250). Her child-like position at her mother's skirt and her screams of "'Mama, Mama'" (250) ironically measure the maturation that has occurred in the woods. Observing the "face of the new misery she felt, but on her mother," Sally Virginia sees what appears in O'Connor's fiction to be the unshakable dominance of patriarchy (250). Come home to her mother and experienced enough now to begin learning from her the adult Southern woman's strategy of compliance to her male counterparts, Sally Virginia is claimed by the Southern patriarchy with an image stunningly similar to the dominant image at the conclusion of "A Temple of the Holy Ghost": both adolescents are marked on their cheeks by the patriarchies—one secular, one religious—that have claimed them.

O'Connor's young females culminate with Mary Grace, a Sally Virginia grown up, able to attack not in the guise of feigned masculine identity, but rather in her own female identity. Although "Revelation" lacks the sexual content of "A Circle in the Fire" and "The Temple of the Holy Ghost," it has not one but two stereotypical mother figures whose notions of raising young girls ironically perpetuate the Southern patriarchy that has restricted their own lives. Accustomed to her mother's constant polite nagging, Mary Grace is driven to radical action by the additional pressures brought to bear on her by Mrs. Turpin. Ruby Turpin's words and demeanor condemn essentially everything about Mary Grace: her acting "ugly," her piercing stares, her acne-blemished complexion, her serious engagement with education. In turn, Mary Grace disdains Ruby Turpin for all of her Southern lady-like postures and their inherent connections to prejudices of class and race. Clearly modeled on Wellesley alumna Maryat Lee, Mary Grace musters the courage to throw the book at Mrs. Turpin because she, like Lee, has managed to escape some of the hold of Southern culture on her.

The emergence of an openly defiant young adult female in one of O'Connor's very late short stories attests to the affect of her friendships with such feminists as Maryat Lee and Betty Hester. In a letter of 21 May 1964,

O'Connor gave Maryat Lee "half interest in Mary Grace" (1209). In a letter two days earlier she had affirmed a reading of the story that Lee had offered:

> Dear Raybucket,
>
> Sure you are right. She gets the vision. Wouldn't have been any point in that story if she hadn't. (1207)

One has to wonder, though, given the world of difference between feminist and agnostic Lee and non-feminist and devout Catholic O'Connor, if the two women would have meant exactly the same thing by the vision in the story. Just as "A Temple of the Holy Ghost" and so much of O'Connor's fiction that supports multiple layers of meaning, "Revelation" invites different although not necessarily contradictory readings. A letter of 25 July 1964 suggests that feminist friend Betty Hester and O'Connor may have debated different readings of the story: "We can worry about the interpitations of Revelation [sic] but not its fortunes. I had a letter from the O'Henry prize people & it got first" (1218).

The authorial intent in "Revelation" is certainly theological: O'Connor strips her protagonist down to such a bare fallen state so that she may recognize her own human frailties as a necessary condition to acceptance of God's grace. In addition to this archetypical Christian theme, Hester and Lee, like other readers willing to look for non-theological access, probably saw in "Revelation" an attack spearheaded by Mary Grace on Southern patriarchy and the middle-aged women whose complicity helps to perpetuate that culture. Gentry has argued that "[i]f O'Connor's characters understood their rebellion against patriarchy, they generally would not want to rebel and could not if they did want to" (61). His claims are certainly true of O'Connor's middle-aged female characters who, although they successfully perform the traditional male work of running farms, still ironically affirm traditional patriarchal gender roles in the upbringing of their children. Gentry's claims, however, do not describe the blatantly defiant young girls of O'Connor's juvenilia or the failed young rebels like the unnamed girl in "The Temple of the Holy Ghost" and Mary Virginia Cope. Nor do those claims allow for an evolution of O'Connor's female characters. As Louise Westling has argued, O'Connor's friendship with Betty Hester (and I would argue with Maryat Lee as well) "helped her to create positive roles for key women characters in the late stories" (15). Certainly Mary Grace from "Revelation" is the penultimate example, defiantly and publicly throwing the book at the patriarchy that attempts to compel her conformity to the niceties and ladylike behaviors O'Connor consistently—if sometime more subtly—attacked in her fiction.

NOTE

1. At the 2001 American Literature Association meeting in Cambridge, MA, Frances Florencourt confirmed to me that O'Connor had worn braces on her teeth for a short time.

WORKS CITED

Driggers, Stephen G. and Robert J. Dunn. *The Manuscripts of Flannery O'Connor at Georgia College*: Athens: U of Georgia P, 1989.

Gentry, Marshall Bruce. "Gender Dialogue in O'Connor." *Flannery O'Connor: New Perspectives*. Ed. Sura P. Rath and Mary Neff Shaw. Athens: U of Georgia P, 1996. 57-72.

Gordon, Sarah. *Flannery O'Connor: The Obedient Imagination*. Athens: U of Georgia P, 2000.

O'Connor, Flannery. *Flannery O'Connor: Collected Works*. Ed. Sally Fitzgerald. New York: Library of America, 1988.

Prown, Katherine Hemple. *Revising Flannery O'Connor: Southern Literary Culture and the Problem of Female Authorship*. Charlottesville: UP of Virginia, 2001.

Westling, Louise. "Flannery O'Connor's Revelations to 'A.'" *Southern Humanities Review* 20 (1986): 15–22.

The Betrayal of Ruby Hill and Hulga Hopewell: Recognizing Feminist Concerns in "A Stroke of Good Fortune" and "Good Country People"

MARGARET D. BAUER

> "The point is not merely to interpret literature in various ways; the point is to *change the world.* We cannot afford to ignore the activity of reading, for it is here that literature is realized as *praxis.* Literature acts on the world by acting on its readers." — Patrocinio P. Schweickart

Very little has been written on Flannery O'Connor's "A Stroke of Good Fortune," and even in what little criticism there is, the role of Ruby's husband Bill Hill as the story's villain has often been overlooked. According to Patrocinio P. Schweickart's reader response theories, as proposed in her essay "Toward a Feminist Theory of Reading," one might suggest that readers have perceived this story, as they do most of O'Connor's fiction, as an androcentric text. Employing Schweickart's methodology, readers would "question their allegiance to text- and author-centered paradigms of criticism" (39) and re-read this story (and other O'Connor stories) from their own feminist perspectives. According to Schweickart,

> The woman reader, now a feminist, embarks on a critical analysis of the reading process, and she realizes that the text has power to structure her experience...However, her recognition of the power of the text is matched by her awareness of her essential role in the process of reading. Without her, the text is nothing—it is inert and harmless. The advent of feminist consciousness and the accompanying commitment to emancipatory *praxis* reconstitutes the subject-object relationship within a dialectical rather than a dualistic framework...The reader can submit to the power of the text, or she can take control of the reading experience. (49)

Applying Schweickart's methodology, I view "the text" as referring to not just O'Connor's stories, but also the body of criticism (with its focus mainly on O'Connor as a Southern Catholic writer) that now influences our reading of those stories. Reading "A Stroke of Good Fortune," for example, from a feminist rather than Christian perspective allows for the recognition of Bill Hill's betrayal of his wife's trust, which, I would argue, is vital to an objective reading of this story, for such a recognition illuminates the story's feminist concerns and thereby renders Ruby a more sympathetic character than she has heretofore been perceived. Ruby does not wish to have children and consequently age before her time, as she witnessed happen to her mother. Trusting her husband, she has left the birth control in his hands, and he has apparently betrayed her.

Similarly, although O'Connor's "Good Country People" has been written about extensively, Mrs. Hopewell's effect upon her daughter—that is, the consequences of her failure to recognize her daughter's value, untraditional though it may be—has to a great extent been ignored. If one reviews Hulga as an individual character, rather than as an O'Connor *type* (the proud intellectual) and, more specifically, considers her as a female character, it becomes significant that readers have excused the behavior of the very traditional Mrs. Hopewell while enjoying the humiliation of her untraditional daughter. Judith Fetterley, author of *The Resisting Reader*, might suggest that women readers' condemnation of Hulga and sympathy for her mother (tempered perhaps by their aggravation with Mrs. Hopewell, but not qualified by Mrs. Hopewell's treatment of her daughter) reflect their own "immasculation": "As readers and teachers and scholars, women are taught to think as men, to identify with a male point of view, and to accept as normal and legitimate a male system of values, one of whose central principles is misogyny" (xx). As a "resisting reader," I would propose a reading of "Good Country People" that recognizes the absence of love and acceptance in Hulga's life and thus allows this proud intellectual to emerge as the more sympathetic character of the two women, but also as much more sympathetic in her own right than she has apparently previously appeared to many readers.

To my surprise and dismay, upon scanning the criticism that has been published about "A Stroke of Good Fortune," I found such summations of the story and its protagonist as the following: Harold C. Gardiner calls this story "perhaps Flannery O'Connor's most purely comic story" (192), and Michel Gresset lists it among "the stories that have more the feel of comedy" (103); neither man qualifies this comment with any recognition that the humor is entirely, even painfully, ironic.[1] Carter W. Martin writes, "the story mocks [Ruby] for the denial of her womanhood" (223), which is the slant of the criticism that I find most distressing in that it suggests that *motherhood* is a requirement for achieving *womanhood.* In *My Mother/My Self,* Nancy Friday discusses the danger of this equation and of related idealizations of the "maternal instinct" (a term Friday uses with reservations): "The maternal instinct says we are all born mothers, that once we are mothers we will automatically and naturally love our children and always do what is best for them. If you believe in the maternal instinct and fail at mother love, you fail as a woman. It is a controlling idea that holds us in an iron grip" (15). Friday then gives her definition of the term, consideration of which might lead readers to a less critical perception of Ruby: "'the maternal instinct' is just this simple liking 'to take care of' smaller creatures. Some human beings do not like it at all. It is not some great biological imperative, which if frustrated will ruin or impoverish a woman's life" (17).[2] Ruby, for example, does not want to have children. Does this make her less of a woman?[3] She remembers that her own mother gave birth to eight children, four of whom died in one way or another. As a consequence of the births, the deaths, and the hard work of raising those who survived, at thirty-four, the age Ruby is at the time of the story, her mother already "looked like a puckered-up old yellow apple, sour, she had always looked sour, she had always looked like she wasn't satisfied with anything" (97).

Of course one might contrast the fact that Ruby is only finding herself pregnant for the first time with her mother having suffered through several pregnancies; and one might also contrast Ruby's economic well-being with her mother's poverty. Ruby's failure to distinguish herself from her mother, however, should not be so surprising. She responds from the experience of having, as an impressionable child—indeed, a daughter who might therefore easily follow in her mother's footsteps—watched her mother suffer the agonies of childbirth and witnessed her mother's sorrow when some pregnancies ended in stillbirth and when some children were lost to illness and accident. Ruby is unable to consider pregnancy without such images of her mother's suffering overcoming her; she has trouble believing that the same could not happen to her. After all, she is her mother's daughter, and both of her sisters, also daughters of this woman, seem to be reliving the nightmare of yearly pregnancies. Significantly, Ruby distinguishes herself among her siblings four paragraphs before mentioning her sisters' pregnancies, whereas *immediately* before making this distinction, she recalls her age and conjures up a picture of her mother at the same age. Evidently, she recognizes the connection even while she tries to deny it, and this recognition seems to dominate, as evidenced by the very fact that she does not consider the possibility that a pregnancy, particularly if it were only one pregnancy, could be different for her than pregnancy was for her mother. Her sisters' recurrent pregnancies seem to suggest to her that once started down that path, one cannot stop; and the end of the path, she believes, is early old age. I therefore find no corroboration in the story for the pregnancy being, as Anthony Di Renzo believes, "the *best*" as well as "the worst thing that can happen to her" (73, my emphasis); nor do I agree with John May's view that "pregnancy promises a renewal of human life" (71). Such a statement is too general; this is not what pregnancy means to every woman—certainly not what it means to Ruby.[4]

Finally, then, although it is true that Ruby apparently does not have as much of an economic struggle as her mother seems to have had, one might consider the possibility that she does not feel that her economic position is secure. Although she views herself as having moved ahead of her family socially, her fourth-floor apartment may leave her distrusting the permanence of this security. If the economics of their household are so stable, why won't Bill Hill provide that house in the suburbs that Ruby desires?[5] Considering this concern about their economic stability, Ruby may feel that at any moment, if she does not control that which she perceives to be in her power to control—her reproductive system—she could turn into her mother.

While we may find Ruby's recognition of her mother's plight more self-centered than sympathetic toward her mother, we are given no reason to doubt the accuracy of her assessment of her mother's life. Considering her mother's suffering, one should be less critical and more understanding of Ruby for not wanting to follow in her mother's footsteps; on the contrary, many of this story's readers have judged Ruby quite harshly. Anthony Di Renzo interprets Ruby's desire to be different as "feel[ing] superior to her illiterate mother" (69). As will be discussed later, this attitude toward Ruby echoes critics like Carter Martin who condemn Joy/Hulga of "Good Country People," for her "pride [and] *her disdain of her home and mother*" (232, my emphasis), among other characteristics. Suffice it to say for now that, looking at such reactions to these two characters together, one should note how they reflect typical reactions to women whose attitudes and ambitions do not reflect and thereby support the norm. Women like Ruby and Hulga threaten the social order and thus are denounced so as not to be perceived as positive role models for others of like minds.

Thus does Dorothy Walters, for example, condemn the "pride and selfishness" reflected in Ruby's "abhorrence of motherhood" (84). Walters believes that Ruby is "reject[ing] her *natural* role as parent" (85, my emphasis). Critics like Walters have apparently accepted the social definition of and belief in "maternal instinct" that concerns Nancy Friday. Friday quotes child psychologist Aaron Esman, who questions the existence of a "maternal instinct": "We have no evidence of it. Women want to become mothers for lots of reasons...but I wouldn't call this 'instinct.'" Among the reasons Esman names: "social expectations; all her life a woman has been expected to grow up, marry and have babies, it's been drummed into her all along, so that her whole orientation is geared toward these expectations from others. But this is not 'maternal instinct'" (qtd. in Friday 19).

Rather than congratulating Ruby for thwarting such expectations, which go against her own desires, these critics condemn her as "unnatural" just because she does not want to be a mother. I would pose the following questions to Walters and to other readers who condemn Ruby on the basis of her wish not to have children: Why can't Ruby have other goals? What is wrong with her goal to move from a fourth-floor apartment to a house? John R. May also mocks this ambition: "So limited is Ruby's selfish perspective that she hopes the 'good fortune' will mean 'moving' to the suburbs where there are no stairs to climb" (71). Apparently also in response to Ruby's desire for a house in the suburbs and her struggle to rise above her rural roots, Anthony Di Renzo calls Ruby "obsessed by wealth and status" (69), an assessment that oversimplifies and belittles Ruby's more serious obsession: not to be drained of her vitality as her mother had been by multiple pregnancies and child raising. I wonder, would readers have found Ruby's desire for a house more acceptable if she also wanted children to raise in that house?

Criticizing Ruby's desperate clinging to the hope that the "stroke of good fortune" in her future is an impending move to the suburbs rather than an impending baby, Marshall Bruce Gentry remarks that Ruby "does little more than make herself ridiculous" (92). Surprisingly, this harsh criticism of Ruby is followed by Gentry's admission that she "attracts some sympathy from readers because she remembers the dreadfulness of her mother's childbearing" (93), a view that is repeated by Suzanne Morrow Paulson: "Her struggle with the facts of her own mortality is worthy of sympathy, however much we may condemn her inability to accept motherhood" (15). It is just such sympathy and recognition of the power of Ruby's memories that keep this reader at least from condemning her—besides the fact that I am not inclined to condemn her in the first place for not wanting to have children. Thus, I disagree with Gentry's suggestion that "[t]he reader is reluctantly forced, consequently, to agree with the narrator's ridicule of [her]" (92–93). Not only do I not find Ruby ridiculous myself, but also I perceive irony, rather than ridicule, in the narrative tone. I would argue that this irony mocks—not Ruby—but the public scorn of the woman who asserts her right not to have children if she does not want them—that is, her right not to fulfill the socially designated role of mother if it does not correspond to her own goals.

Whether O'Connor intended the irony I perceive in the tone and, if she did, whether she was directing the irony toward society rather than her protagonist is not an issue for a reader-response reading such as this one. As Patrocinio Schweickart reminds us, "the validity of an interpretation cannot be decided by appealing to what the author 'intended,' to what is 'in' the text, or to what is 'in' the experience of the reader," the latter of which qualification will answer those readers who question my reading on the basis of their experience of O'Connor's fiction, experience which may be based on perceiving her work as androcentric. Schweickart continues, "We can think of validity not as a property inherent in an interpretation, but rather as a *claim* implicit in the *act* of propounding an interpretation. An interpretation, then, is not valid or invalid in itself. Its validity is contingent on the agreement of others" (56). Thus, my reading does not ask others to believe that O'Connor meant her readers to pity Ruby or meant to mock the public who would scorn Ruby; rather, I would suggest that readers with feminist sensibilities apply them to Ruby's situation. Doing so, I believe, will lead readers to a similar perception of Ruby's sympathetic appeal.

I do recognize that it is quite obvious throughout the story that Ruby is in a serious state of denial regarding her apparent pregnancy; however, I would not agree that this denial makes her appear "ridiculous." Nor do I "condemn her inability to accept motherhood" (Paulson 15). Quite the contrary: it is the extent of her denial that makes her a sympathetic, even pitiful character. In the course of the story, she struggles against facing two devastating truths: one, that she is pregnant, which, to her, is a death sentence; and two, that her husband has betrayed her.[6] Given these ultimate revelations, it is also surprising to me that Dorothy Walters has remarked that the story "is unusual in the O'Connor canon in that nothing of a truly catastrophic nature occurs" during the "movement…toward revelation" (86). Perhaps not, in Walters's estimation of events, but to Ruby—and to readers who recognize the serious nature of oppressive ideals of womanhood—the realization of her pregnancy and, perhaps more significantly, of her husband's betrayal would qualify as "catastrophic."

Indeed, the narrator hints that Bill Hill has intentionally and deviously gotten his wife pregnant against her expressed will. I consider this betrayal to be the most devastating revelation in the story. Early in the story the reader is made aware that, in spite of Ruby's belief that she, unlike her mother, controls her life, it is actually her husband Bill Hill who is in charge—of everything from the couple's residence to Ruby's body. This fact becomes first apparent in Ruby's dissatisfaction with their apartment. She wants to move to a subdivision, but Bill has apparently not yet agreed to the move, and apparently, it is his decision to make. Second, the reader is repeatedly informed that Bill "takes care of" the couple's birth control during their sexual relations. In further ruminations as she climbs the stairs, Ruby congratulates herself on having "no children, all that *by herself.* She would have had five children by now if *she* hadn't been careful" (98, my emphasis). In truth, as she later reveals during her conversation with her neighbor Laverne, "Bill Hill takes care of that" (104). Evidently, under the guise of taking responsibility for birth control, Bill Hill has assumed control of Ruby's body—and he seems to have ultimately exerted and thereby exploited his control by impregnating Ruby against her wishes. It becomes clear that, as Laverne puts it, "old Bill Hill just slipped up about four or five months ago" (104), and that this "slip-up" was probably intentional.

In her discussion of reading Ruby as a "bad Catholic," Joanne McMullen focuses on "Bill Hill's "slip-up" as "provid[ing] the catalyst to compel Ruby to an adherence to the Catholic meaning of marriage, procreation" (88). Like other critics, McMullen focuses solely upon finding fault with Ruby for not wanting children and leaves out Bill Hill's participation in the "mortal sin" of using birth control: "Readers would have little trouble interpreting *Ruby's* tacit agreement to interfere with the life-giving potential of the sexual act as a deliberate flaunting of the Catholic rules concerning birth control that places *Ruby's* soul in spiritual jeopardy" (McMullen 88, my emphasis). Readings that leave Bill out of the equation as they direct their condemnation upon Ruby alone are disturbingly reminiscent of Milton's emphasis of Eve's guilt for the fall of *man*. Bill Hill's "slip-up" is a serious breach of faith with his wife, particularly given her feelings about children and motherhood, of which he must be aware: as the reader has witnessed, Ruby is quite forthright about her feelings on these subjects

Looking back, then, the reader finds evidence that Ruby is slowly realizing that her husband has betrayed her and that, as a result, she is pregnant. The first hint of her subconscious knowledge comes when, tiring during her climb upstairs, she sits down on the steps to rest and lands on a neighbor boy's toy pistol, a blatantly phallic image. The reference to the gun as "nine inches of *treacherous* tin" reveals Ruby's subconscious recognition that her husband has betrayed her (98, my emphasis). One can further infer from Ruby's recollection of Bill's recent inexplicable happiness that he has planned Ruby's pregnancy, since his attitude suggests that he knows she is pregnant before she does. After her altercation with Laverne, Ruby considers her recent weight-gain and comforts herself with the thought that "Bill Hill didn't mind her being fat" (105). However, continuing her thoughts, this seeming testimony of his unconditional love for her becomes, rather, testimony of his intentional betrayal: "She saw Bill Hill's long happy face, grinning at her from the eyes downward in a way he had as if his look got happier as it neared his teeth" (105). Anthony Di Renzo, one of the few critics to discuss Ruby's husband to any extent, equates the smile with the grin of the Cheshire cat and "the cat that swallowed the canary," also suggesting that Bill planned this unwanted pregnancy—or, as Di Renzo puts it, that "Ruby has been railroaded" (72). Louise Westling remarks on the smile, too, which, she argues, "grows slyer and slyer" in retrospect, "so that by the end we know Ruby made a mistake in trusting him" (149). Juxtaposed against the description of Bill's recent smiling is Ruby's sudden, seemingly unrelated thought, "He would never slip up" (105), which reveals her desire to deny the evidence before her of her husband's treachery.[7] Ruby then again dismisses the possibility that she is pregnant with the insistence to herself that "she was just fat" (105), which, if the case, would reflect the genuineness of Bill's love for her in that his smile is proof that he does not mind her weight gain—as opposed to the falseness of his love if he has betrayed her and smiles because he knows she is pregnant. She soon returns, however, to the thought that "Bill Hill couldn't have slipped up," adding this time, first, her husband's reassurance that "it [which apparently refers to their method of birth control] was guaranteed," and second, her own experience that "it had worked all this time," to try to convince herself that she is not pregnant and therefore that her husband has not been so deceitful—and selfish—after all (106).

Having followed the progression of Ruby's thoughts, the reader should realize that her despair at the end of the story is not only a result of facing the fact that she is pregnant; it is also despair at the thought of how her husband, to whom she has literally entrusted her life (since she associates pregnancy with death), has betrayed her trust in favor of his own desires. It is this despair that undermines the comic elements of the story for me and that allows Ruby to be considered a sympathetic character in spite of her snobbery and blindness. Her snobbery has evolved from her desire not to follow in her mother's footsteps to an early grave, as her sisters are doing, each having had a baby per year since their marriages. Indeed, I find a kind of admirable courage in Ruby's defiance of traditional gender roles. And her blindness to her condition is certainly understandable, given not only her association of children and death, but also due to the implications about her husband's character and priorities that can be derived from her unwanted pregnancy—that is, that her desires are not to be considered when they conflict with his.

Perhaps one might argue that Ruby has been selfish in her decision not to have children in that, as far as the reader knows from the content of the story, she has not inquired about Bill Hill's view on the subject; that is, in the course of the story, she does not reflect back to any time when she asked him if he wanted children. But neither does she reflect back upon any time that he expressed a desire for children. On the other hand, she makes no secret of her wish to remain childless. If he wanted a child, why didn't he speak up? In any case, what makes her refusal to fulfill his desire any more reprehensible than his betrayal of her? If both are guilty of insensitivity to their spouse's desires, the question I expressed earlier must again be asked: why is she the only one of the two who receives so many readers' scorn?

Leon V. Driskell and Joan T. Brittain suggest that this story follows the pattern of other O'Connor stories in which a negatively depicted character experiences some kind of epiphany that will lead to the achievement of Grace. They argue that "[Ruby's] realization of her unborn child as a force outside her...suggests her release from the purely physical and mortal concerns which obsess her at the story's opening. Her recognition of life is linked to awareness of death; her mind is on the eternal, not the temporal, when the story ends" (73). Although I find the possibility of such hopefulness for Ruby appealing, I do not perceive its presence in O'Connor's description of the baby waiting "out *nowhere* in *nothing*"; Ruby seems to me to be threatened still by the baby "resting and waiting, with plenty of time" (107, my emphasis).

In spite of her efforts to escape her mother's fate, Ruby ultimately decides she is doomed to just that, as indicated by the final image of her peering through the prison-like bars of the staircase's banister, crying out in despair as she feels the new life move inside of her, a life that she believes will drain her of her own vitality. How could one not sympathize with this caged woman? And how could one view this story as comic? I would argue that its ending is one of the darkest in O'Connor's canon.

With this more generous, less judgmental attitude toward O'Connor's somewhat (on the surface) disagreeable protagonists, I turn now to the story "Good Country People." Just as Bill Hill's betrayal of his wife has been downplayed as critics focus their judgment upon Ruby, I found only one critic, Richard Giannone, who recognizes that Mrs. Hopewell's treatment of her daughter may have played a role in the evolution of Joy into Hulga. I hasten to qualify my agreement with this reading of Mrs. Hopewell's responsibility for "Hulga." Like recent criticism that re-reads Faulkner's Caroline Compson, who has traditionally been blamed for the eventual destruction of all of the Compson children,[8] I would argue that analysis of the patriarchal social structure of this story's setting provides a similar defense of Mrs. Hopewell's treatment of her daughter. Such an analysis lies outside of the realm of this paper, but before I proceed with an exploration of Mrs. Hopewell's role in shaping her daughter's character, I will defend Mrs. Hopewell on some of the same bases that I defended Ruby Hill. Referring again to Nancy Friday's discussion of false notions of "maternal instinct": "We are raised to believe that mother love is different from other kinds of love. It is not open to error, doubt, or to the ambivalence of ordinary affections. This is an illusion" (3). As will be shown to be the case with Mrs. Hopewell, "Mothers…sometimes do not like [their children]" (Friday 3). Such negative feelings about one's own child should be considered no more "unnatural" than not wanting to have a child.

Yet one cannot deny the negative effect of a disapproving parent upon a child. Although many critics have recognized that Mrs. Hopewell is not very appealing herself, they have not pursued the effect of her character upon her daughter's.[9] Most critics have focused their attention instead upon condemning Hulga for, as listed by Carter Martin, her "pride, her disdain of her home and mother, her vanity concerning her leg, and her Ph.D. in philosophy," all of which, according to Martin, preclude any sympathetic response to the early tragic loss of Joy's leg in a hunting accident (232). Given this condemnation of Hulga's pride, critics tend to view the story's end as poetic justice. However, I share instead Carol Schloss's reaction to the story's conclusion:

> Although it is an old story of the fox and the chicken, of the trickster cunningly outwitted, there is no surprised delight at the outcome. The issues of good and evil are obscure, the result of the "rape" [referring to Manley taking Hulga's leg] too peculiarly jarring, the characters too distantly rendered at the point of greatest vulnerability to effect a pleasurable sense of the tables turned. (43)

Schloss's rape analogy suggests that her feminist sensibilities influenced her response to the story. More readers might consider examining this story from a feminist perspective rather than just through the Christian lenses more typically employed during an analysis of O'Connor's fiction. Such re-visioning would illuminate how Hulga's supposedly proud nature, condemned by Christian sensibilities, can be viewed as a mask for her insecurity.

To begin a re-evaluation of Hulga's sympathetic appeal, one should note O'Connor's first hint, provided within the sentence structure of the following passage, that Mrs. Hopewell's assessment of her daughter's behavior is not to be considered reliable: "When Hulga stumped into the kitchen in the morning (she could walk without making the awful noise but she made it—Mrs. Hopewell was certain—because it was ugly-sounding), she glanced at them and did not speak" (275). Notice that O'Connor qualifies the possibility of Hulga's deliberation in making the noise that disturbs her mother: "Mrs. Hopewell was certain" that Hulga could control "the awful noise." That is not to say that it is so, however. Perhaps, in truth, Hulga actually cannot help making the noise. This possibility suggests a pettiness in Mrs. Hopewell's response to her daughter's tragic early loss: she is selfishly disturbed by the "ugliness" of Hulga's condition. This pettiness somewhat undermines Mrs. Hopewell's earlier expression of sympathy for her daughter's condition: "it tore her heart to think…of the poor stout girl in her thirties who had never danced a step or had any normal good times" (274). Richard Giannone—again, the one critic who seems to acknowledge Mrs. Hopewell's share of the responsibility for her daughter's behavior—perceives in Mrs. Hopewell a "shame over the girl's loss, reinforced by pitying niceties"; he argues that this shame "produces in Joy a similar sense of shame at her failure to be the girl she is supposed to be" (63). Still, Hulga is a proud woman, so she covers this shame with what I suggest is false bravado rather than arrogance—hence, her surly attitude.

Mrs. Hopewell's annoyance upon hearing her daughter "stump" into the kitchen in the morning also leads one to recognize the implications behind the reason for her concern about her daughter's Ph.D. First of all, the advanced degree puts Mrs. Hopewell in the awkward position of having to explain her daughter's vocation to those who inquire: "You could say, 'My daughter is a nurse,' or 'My daughter is a schoolteacher,' or even, 'My daughter is a chemical engineer.' You could not say, 'My daughter is a philosopher'" (276). Second, Mrs. Hopewell's dismay about Hulga having completed her studies so that "now…there was no more excuse for her to go to school again" (276) sounds very much like she does not want her daughter around. Of course, not relishing her daughter's company is understandable given Hulga's disposition. And, given my support for Ruby's right not to want children, I do not here mean to hold Mrs. Hopewell to such stereotypical expectations as unconditional love for her child, but I do find it interesting that readers have been troubled by Ruby's lack of the supposedly natural desire in women for children, but not by Mrs. Hopewell's attitude toward her daughter.

Throughout this paper, I have referred to Nancy Friday's points of concern regarding unrealistic expectations, caused by social acceptance of the "maternal instinct," a term she uses in much the same way I use the phrase "unconditional love." I have employed this material to encourage readers to recognize the effects of such socialization upon women's self-esteem and thereby to be more sympathetic toward the predicament of those women who find themselves considered "bad mothers" or "unnatural women." Here, I turn to the effects of such socialization upon the children. As Friday explains, "Children think their parents are perfect, and if anything is wrong it's their fault" (8). Mothers like Mrs. Hopewell, with her optimistic maxims for every occasion, who cannot admit to having negative feelings about their children, suggest to their children, and to the world at large, that the negativity is all one-sided and thus that all the fault for the problematic relationship lies with the child. Therefore, while I support Friday's perception of "the tyranny of the notion of maternal instinct [that] idealizes motherhood beyond human capacity" (16), I still sympathize with the other victims of this "tyranny": the children who do not receive the unconditional love their socialization leads them to expect from their mothers.

Unconditional love is an ideal that asks too much of mothers. Assessing Mrs. Hopewell's love is not the agenda of this discussion of the story. I am more concerned about Mrs. Hopewell's inability to accept her daughter's difference from, for example, Mrs. Freeman's daughters with their traditional lives (one already married and pregnant, the other with an active social life). Certainly Hulga—first pursuing a graduate degree rather than a husband while in college and now, unmarried at thirty-two—is unique among the women her age in this rural Southern community. One suspects from the ambition and interests implicit in her pursuit of this graduate degree that Hulga would stand out among her local peers even if she had not lost her leg. Mrs. Hopewell's pity for "this poor stout girl in her thirties" and grief that Hulga "never danced a step or had any *normal* good times" suggests that her concern is more about Hulga not being "normal" than about Hulga's heart problem or lost limb—or about her unhappiness, which is reflected in her disposition (274, my emphasis).

The reader of "Good Country People" might then wonder if the lack of the kind of security provided by knowing one has at least her mother's support has anything to do with Hulga's disposition. One can find corroboration for such a reading in the earlier report of Hulga's remark to her mother, "If you want me, here I am—LIKE I AM," a response to her mother's implicit rejection of her daughter's offensiveness as she sets conditions for Hulga's company: "If you can't come pleasantly, I don't want you at all" (274).[10] Certainly one can understand why Mrs. Hopewell would not find her walks through her fields very enjoyable with her daughter sulking and making rude comments the whole time. At the same time, one can see how these words can also be interpreted as a more general rejection of her daughter due to Hulga's overall unpleasantness, particularly her failure to be more like Mrs. Freeman's daughters, whom Mrs. Hopewell refers to as "two of the finest girls she knew"; however, unlike Glynese, Hulga has no "admirers" and therefore, unlike Carramae, no prospects of soon being "married and pregnant" (272). Hulga must be aware of her "difference" from other daughters, and she seems to be expressing her wish to be accepted—at least by her mother—in spite of these differences.

Again, however, one should not expect Mrs. Hopewell to love, or even for that matter to like, such a disagreeable woman just because that woman is her daughter. Hulga is, after all, something of a monster, at least according to the majority of critics of this story. I wonder, though, how did Hulga become such an adult? As the reader of Faulkner's *The Sound and the Fury* has witnessed, doting on one's child, as Mrs. Compson dotes on Jason, can produce a monster even more disturbing than Hulga. But so, apparently, can withholding such attention from one's child, showing no acceptance or approval at all of his or her actions and aspirations. If the absence of an accepting, supportive mother is not what created Hulga's attitude, it certainly does nothing to change it. Therefore, "Good Country People" is not only an indictment of Hulga's pride. One might also examine the story from Hulga's perspective to try to determine why she behaves as she does and perhaps thereby to perceive what else O'Connor might be criticizing.[11]

Looking at the situation from the eyes of the character whose behavior is displeasing to the reader is something I ask my students to do whenever they are too quick to denounce a character—Edna of Kate Chopin's *The Awakening*, Calixta of Chopin's "The Storm," Toni Morrison's Sula, to name a few of the characters students are quickest to criticize (and one might notice that they are all women who defy traditional roles). I would add to this list, though she does not come up as often, Washington Irving's Dame Van Winkle and credit Judith Fetterley's reading of "Rip Van Winkle" with calling my attention to the problematic reader response that labels this character a shrew when all she wants is her husband to expend some of his energy working at home rather than exerting himself helping neighbors and then neglecting his own home's needs (thus, significantly, her condemned behavior results from her efforts to get her husband to fulfill his traditional role). Interestingly, the last time I taught *The Sound and the Fury*, students were quicker to defend Jason Compson as the product of a dysfunctional family than I have found students willing to "forgive" the female characters I have listed above. In light of this odd defense of one of the most reprehensible characters in fiction, I would point out here that, even as I explain Hulga's behavior, I do not necessarily mean to excuse it.

Like Jason Compson, Hulga is an adult, and at some point the adult must be held responsible for her own behavior (as opposed to blaming the parents). Thus, I would agree with recent feminist critics who defend Caroline Compson, but I would take this defense further than explaining her behavior and considering perspective before condemning her. I would remind readers that regardless of how much his mother's hypochondria, class consciousness, and spoiling formed Jason's character, he is still accountable for his treatment of his sister, niece, and servants. Again, then, my argument above is not meant to condemn Mrs. Hopewell but rather to explain Hulga's negative attitude. I do not find a contradiction between my continued condemnation of Jason and my defense of Hulga because Hulga does not so torment those around her as Jason does his family and servants. Unlike Jason, too, Hulga reaches out for love when it finally seems that it is being offered to her. This point of contrast further reflects why she has sympathetic appeal while he seems irredeemable. My reading of O'Connor is therefore directly in the tradition of Fetterley's theories of being a "resisting reader." I am asking readers to "resist" the typical—or traditional—readings of "Good Country People" and "A Stroke of Good Fortune" and re-view these stories from the protagonists' perspectives.

Given Hulga's academic achievements, it is arguable that she is quite capable of perceiving her mother's disappointment in her and of understanding the reasons why she does not please her mother. As Martha Chew has discussed, Hulga's intellect, as much as her missing leg, keeps her from being the traditional Southern belle daughter. Even Chew, who I believe has offered the best reading of the story, fails either to recognize or to acknowledge the probable effects that perceiving that her own mother does not accept her has had on Hulga's emotional well-being, when social conditioning would tell Hulga that her mother is the one person from whom she might expect acceptance. For even if unconditional love is an ideal that one should not expect of the mother, it is true that the child who does not receive evidence of the mother's love (through acceptance and approval) suffers from the rejection. Consider the case of children put up for adoption who spend their lives wondering what was so wrong with them that their birth mothers didn't want them.

Realizing Hulga's sense of rejection should provide the reader with a clearer understanding of how she came to turn to the young man who calls himself Manley Pointer and how she could have been so blind to his duplicity when she is usually capable of discerning the hypocrisy of others. The absence of love, support, or even just acceptance in Hulga's life also renders her encounter with Manley and his humiliation of her much less comic than perceived by some readers. Before he reveals his true nature, Manley appears to recognize the admirable and even tender qualities that Mrs. Hopewell cannot see beneath Hulga's discomforting surface: he calls her "brave" and "sweet" and gives her a look of "complete admiration" (283). He tells Hulga that he is able to perceive her true value because he is "'not like these people that a serious thought don't ever enter their heads...because [he] may die'" (284). Hulga's empathetic response to his remark—that she "may die too" (284)—suggests not only that she is trying to establish a bond between herself and another person, but also that she is looking for someone who would be sorry, who would miss her, when she dies.[12] Although I am not suggesting that Mrs. Hopewell would not mourn her daughter, one can imagine Hulga believing that her mother would only be relieved by her death.

Thus begins Hulga's fantasy of joining her life with this kindred sufferer who recognizes her value. Therefore, when Manley remarks again upon Hulga's attractive uniqueness during their exchange the next day in the hayloft, and in so doing reveals fascination with rather than disgust for her wooden leg (which, as suggested, is a manifestation of the perception of her uniqueness as a handicap rather than an asset), she is ready to commit herself to him: "She was thinking that she would run away with him and that every night he would take the leg off and every morning put it back on again" (289). This fantasy, as David Eggenschwiler interprets it, reflects Hulga's "neurotically sublimated sexuality, her desire to relax her defenses, and her need to admit dependence" (56); Dorothy Tuck McFarland suggests that during their encounter Hulga reveals that she "has not given up on the possibility of love" (37). One can infer from Hulga's fantasy that she would perhaps like to live a more "normal" life after all, if that is what it takes to be loved. She would conform herself to fit into the more traditional role of dependent woman in return for intimacy and acceptance.[13] One might again turn to Eggenschwiler to understand why she dares to take this risk with Manley, when she did not dare to do so with her mother: "Faced with what seemed to be an adoring, childlike boy, Hulga felt safe enough to experience emotions that she had previously protected herself against" (57). Ironically and unfortunately, the disingenuous Manley was actually sincere about being attracted to Hulga's difference. Therefore, once she betrays her "common" desire for the love of "good country people" (like her mother), he becomes disenchanted with her and runs off with her leg.[14] Hulga is then left with her recognition of a desire for love and no person from whom she can expect it, for her mother has experienced no similar enlightenment about her daughter's secret needs, and none is foreseeable.

Critics so often limit their attention to the Christian or Southern themes in O'Connor's stories that her feminist themes have been overlooked. In these two stories, for example, O'Connor presents the trials of women who have attempted to reject traditional roles in search of a more fulfilling life but who have been ultimately forced into conforming their lives to fulfill more "proper" roles for women: Ruby is tricked into becoming a mother; Hulga is seduced into accepting dependency. O'Connor's harshness in her characterization of these protagonists seems to have resulted in readers failing to see how the people in their lives have to some extent caused them to act the way they do. One might keep in mind that O'Connor herself remarked in a letter to "A" that she tended "to throw the weight of circumstance against the character I favor" (*Habit of Being* 120–21). Thus, one should not take her harsh characterizations as indicating that she meant to condemn these women. Readers need to examine the role of the minor characters more carefully so as not to view Hulga as unsympathetically as Mrs. Hopewell does or not to fail to see the tragic significance of Bill Hill's betrayal of his wife in forcing her to have his child and reveling in this sign of his domination over Ruby.

I wonder at critics' failure to look at these two stories from a different perspective, especially since those perspectives are the main characters', which leads me to wonder about the tendency to pigeon-hole O'Connor as a Catholic and a Southern writer, the consequence of which seems to be that the characters—and the author—are treated as though they are asexual—out of the realm of sexuality and thus of gender concerns.[15] Indeed, this may be a reason that O'Connor was welcomed into the canon so quickly, while many of her female contemporaries and predecessors have only relatively recently been anthologized, even acknowledged. As Patrocinio Schweickart notes, "An androcentric canon generates androcentric interpretive strategies, which in turn favor the canonization of androcentric texts and the marginalization of gynocentric ones" (45). Fred Hobson has pointed out that "[i]n the twentieth century…a certain *kind* of white women [writers] were never really excluded" from the Southern literary canon (74). Hobson includes O'Connor among the women he lists and argues that "these women were accepted because…they did not truly challenge the patriarchal southern system…or were not perceived to at the time, in any substantial way" (74). One can certainly see how O'Connor would pose no threat since her fiction does not overtly associate her criticism of the South with its patriarchy. Even her depictions of racism are usually toward the purpose of negatively characterizing someone in a story (his or her racism reflects his or her individual narrow-mindedness and shallowness) rather than the system in general, as it has evolved from the Old South.

O'Connor, in other words, did not discomfort her readers in the way that such writers as Kate Chopin and Zora Neale Hurston did. She discomforts readers on a spiritual—again an asexual— level. This is not at all meant to be a criticism of O'Connor's fiction. O'Connor's chief concerns were spiritual, not feminist in nature, and I do not mean to suggest that as a woman she had a responsibility to write feminist literature. But neither should one hold that her primary focus on spiritual issues precludes any feminist concerns. As Sarah Gordon suggests, "even as we grant O'Connor her theological point, we may find also a social one: writing from her own knowledge and experience of mannered southern society, O'Connor is greatly concerned with questions of female power and control" (119). Whether intended or not, stories like "A Stroke of Good Fortune" and "Good Country People" do deal with feminist themes: in the first, a woman's right to choose not to be a mother, not to fulfill that role if it does not suit her to do so; and in the second, the awkwardness of being an intellectual woman, of thereby also not fulfilling the preferred social construct, in this case preferred by her mother rather than her husband. The extent to which any of O'Connor's many strong female characters actually controls the home or husband she seems to dominate might be deconstructed on the basis of a feminist analysis of the underlying patriarchy that these women's positions of power defy. One might reconsider their falls, then, not only from the religious perspective of how their destruction is a result of pride, that first, most deadly of sins, but also as reflective of attempts to undermine, even punish, such thwarting of the patriarchy.

NOTES

1. A much more accurate assessment of the tone of the story can be derived from Anthony Di Renzo's comparison of Ruby's reactions in the story to one's reactions to the experiences of a carnival: "The same principle of surprise, degradation, and physical assault operates at carnivals. Rides and games, rich food and blaring music shock and trick us into confronting our bodies. Our hearts beat faster, we sweat, we throw up, and the experience is both amusing and menacing" (71). I would argue that this analogy also applies to one's reactions upon reading this story.
2. Of course, Ruby is a character in a story, not a human being, and, as Margaret and Michael Rustin point out, "Many modern literary critics have

become hypercritical of the supposed realist fallacy of imagining fictional characters as real, and attributing motives and histories to them beyond what is actually stated” (14). I agree with the Rustins, however, that if characters “cannot be responded to as plausible representations of some reality, whether internal or external, whether of the writer’s or some other people’s experience, they will seem to have little point or connection with the reader’s world” (14–15). Therefore, in this essay, I will “write about characters as if they possessed all the complex and interrelated feelings of actual people” and “mak[e] inferences which are appropriate to analytic psychotherapy” (as I have just done in applying Friday’s theories to Ruby), believing, as the Rustins do, “that authors have imagined situations and persons *as if* they were real…have made connections between the different events of their story and the feelings of their characters with an intuitive grasp of the way people thus imagined are or would be” (14).

3. Whether it makes her less of a Catholic is, I would argue, not relevant since O’Connor gives no indication within the story that Ruby is a Catholic. However, I direct readers who question my not reading the story in a Catholic context—that is, by viewing Ruby’s not wanting children from the perspective of the Catholic Church—to Joanne Halleran McMullen’s chapter on “Catholic Themes in the Works of O’Connor,” perhaps the most sympathetic reading of Ruby to date. Indeed, like me, McMullen believes that Ruby “may be more due our compassion than our condemnation.” McMullen begins this chapter noting that “O’Connor had a certain aversion to being perceived as simply a Catholic writer and, therefore, a writer expected to have a plainly orthodox agenda” (79), quoting from letters in *The Habit of Being* for support. McMullen opens her discussion of “A Stroke of Good Fortune” by calling it “one of O’Connor’s most explicit endorsements of Catholic doctrine”—in that Ruby suffers for her “very un-Catholic attitude” of not wanting children, “since a Catholic marriage is not considered consummated until the sexual act has been performed, and this act must never dictate to God by thwarting the prospect of procreation” (85). However, then McMullen shows how the story “rail[s] against motherhood by making constant and inconsistent references to its trials and tribulations,” given which, while Ruby may be “a bad Catholic…her resistance to childbirth [is] a…humanly understandable response” (86). While McMullen understands—and shows—how readers find that the story corroborates O’Connor’s support of the Catholic position regarding birth control (88), she concludes her discussion of the story arguing, “The

problem in perceiving this as a Catholic story is precisely that Ruby never stands condemned for holding ideas contrary to Catholic teachings… This O'Connor story does not instruct us about how a Catholic wife should behave in a proper Catholic marriage; it shows us a frightened woman forced into precisely the terrifying hole she wanted to escape" (89).

4. Joanne McMullen's remarks about the negative depiction of motherhood, quoted in note 3, are more recognizable, as is Claire Kahane's reading of the meaning of childbirth in this story (except for her perception of its depiction as comical): "childbirth is presented by O'Connor as a radical mutilation, a martyrdom to the species which the story reifies in Ruby's Calvary-like ascent up the stairs, her cross no less burdensome for its comic portrayal" (246).

5. It is interesting to note that critics who view Ruby's failure to desire children as a failure to fulfill her role as a wife and/or woman do not similarly perceive Bill's failure to buy the house that Ruby desires as a failure to fulfill his traditional role as "provider"; thus, critics have not condemned Bill for that breach of "contract" as they have Ruby for resisting her role as mother.

6. Kathleen Hemple Prown points out an interesting revision from the original version of this story, which was cut from the novel *Wise Blood* (Ruby was Hazel Motes's sister, who was trying to get an abortion). According to Prown,

> the passages concerning Ruby's abortion sympathetically explore the tragic consequences of unwanted pregnancy and offer a pointed critique of the male treachery that functions as a mere subtext in the published version of Ruby's story…[t]he two stories figure her situation in different ways—in the published version, as the inevitable destiny to which embodiment assigns women, and in the original version, as the problematic result of male treachery and exploitation. (123)

Prown interprets Ruby's death at the end of the original version, "not as punishment for her wayward sexuality but as the tragic result of the misuse of male authority" (124).

7. Claire Kahane also suggests that Bill Hill's "slip up" means he has "betrayed her" (246). One might defend Bill to some extent on the basis that he, too, would have been fed the social definition of "maternal instinct" that Friday discusses. But even so, his actions support Friday's contention that "[w]omen must have this myth taken off their backs. It puts them at the

mercy of a male chauvinistic society. Men are 'sure' that women are meant to be mothers… Male supremacy uses the myth of the maternal instinct to reinforce its power position" (17).

8. See, for example, Joan Williams's "In Defense of Caroline Compson."
9. One exception is Ralph C. Wood, who, like other critics, points out that Hulga's "human audience consists of two grossly complacent creatures, her mother and the tenant farm woman." In contrast to other critics, however, he argues that, consequently, "[o]ne must be careful not to judge [her] as a totally unsympathetic character, for she has considerable cause for discontent" (101).
10. I therefore find no basis for Rose Bowen's reading of Hulga's remark as an egotistical association of herself with "the 'I AM' who spoke to Moses (Exodus 3:14) and the *ego eimi* (John 8:58) who declared 'before Abraham came to be, I AM.'" Bowen is apparently criticizing Hulga's audacity in "tak[ing] on an omnipotence akin to idolatry in setting herself up as supreme" (94). This reading is unfounded. Hulga seems, rather, to be asserting her right to be a flawed daughter.
11. O'Connor has indicated in her prose that she perceived Hulga as "spiritually as well as physically crippled" and that she interprets the ending as suggesting that Manley Pointer has "revealed [Hulga's] deeper *affliction* to her for the first time" (*Mystery and Manners* 99, my emphasis). However, given O'Connor's remarks in this same essay regarding having had no set agenda when she sat down to write this (or any) story, one should recognize that the Christian agenda found in much of her fiction is not the only level of interpretation.
12. The reader is here reminded that "[t]he doctors had told Mrs. Hopewell that with the best of care, Joy might see forty-five. She had a weak heart" (276). One might consider, in light of my sympathetic reading of Hulga, her "weak heart" to be as symbolic as it is physical—like the "heart trouble" that Chopin mentions when characterizing the protagonist of "The Story of an Hour" and the "heart disease" that kills this character at the end of the story. Mrs. Mallard's "heart trouble," the reader realizes as Chopin's story develops, is a spiritual malaise that results from dissatisfaction with her life.
13. Frederick Asals also apparently sees Hulga's fantasy of Manley taking off and putting on her leg each night and morning as a sign that she is willing to be dependent upon someone, though he calls it "an image of marriage *inter*dependence, a merging of the knowledge of Hulga with the innocence of Manley" (103).

14. Given my earlier reference to Toni Morrison's Sula, it is interesting to note here that Morrison has Sula experience a similar rejection from a man when she begins to behave like other women: her lover Ajax, who had been attracted to "her elusiveness and indifference to established habits of behavior" (127), leaves her when she behaves "like all of her sisters before her" (133).
15. In contrast to typical critical reception to the seemingly asexuality of O'Connor's writing, Patricia Smith Yaeger perceives O'Connor the writer as having "attempted…to remain in the tomboyish role of the angel-aggressive little girl" in order to express her anger at the system. Yaeger implies that writing as a woman—more specifically, a Southern woman—she might repress her anger: "rather than acting flirtatious or womanly, rather than upholding her community's norms by withholding her aggression, she begins to attack her society's angels; she picks up her pen and starts to write" (96).

WORKS CITED

Asals, Frederick. "The Double." *Modern Critical Views: Flannery O'Connor*. Ed. Harold Bloom. New York: Chelsea, 1986. 93–110.

Bowen, Rose, O. P. "Baptism by Inversion." *Flannery O'Connor Bulletin* 14 (1985): 94–98.

Chew, Martha. "Flannery O'Connor's Double-Edged Satire: The Idiot Daughter versus the Lady Ph.D." *Southern Quarterly* 19.2 (1981): 17–25.

Di Renzo, Anthony. *American Gargoyles: Flannery O'Connor and the Medieval Grotesque*. Carbondale: Southern Illinois UP, 1993.

Driskell, Leon V., and Joan T. Brittain. *The Eternal Crossroads: The Art of Flannery O'Connor*. UP of Kentucky, 1971.

Eggenschwiler, David. *The Christian Humanism of Flannery O'Connor*. Detroit: Wayne State UP, 1972.

Fetterley, Judith. *The Resisting Reader: A Feminist Approach to American Fiction*. Bloomington: Indiana UP, 1978.

Friday, Nancy. *My Mother/My Self: The Daughter's Search for Identity*. 1977. New York: Delacorte, 1987.

Gardiner, Harold C., S. J. "Flannery O'Connor's Clarity of Vision." *The Added Dimension: The Art and Mind of Flannery O'Connor*. Eds. Melvin J. Fieldman and Lewis A. Lawson. New York: Fordham UP, 1966.

Gentry, Marshall Bruce. *Flannery O'Connor: Religion of the Grotesque*. Jackson: UP of Mississippi, 1986.

Giannone, Richard. *Flannery O'Connor and the Mystery of Love*. Urbana: U of Illinois P, 1989.

Gordon, Sarah. "'The Crop': Limitation, Restraint, and Possibility." *Flannery O'Connor: New Perspectives*. Ed. Sura P. Rath and Mary Neff Shaw. Athens: U of Georgia P, 1996. 96–120.

Gresset, Michel. "The Audacity of Flannery O'Connor." Translated by T. G. Bernard-West. *Critical Essays on Flannery O'Connor*. Eds. Melvin J. Friedman and Beverly Lyon Clark. Boston: Hall, 1985. 100–08.

Hobson, Fred. "Of Canons and Cultural Wars: Southern Literature and Literary Scholarship after Midcentury." *The Future of Southern Letters*. Ed. Jefferson Humphries and John Lowe. New York: Oxford UP, 1996. 72–86.

Kahane, Claire. "The Maternal Legacy: The Grotesque Tradition in Flannery O'Connor's Female Gothic." *The Female Gothic*. Ed. Juliann E. Fleenor. Montreal: Eden, 1983. 242–56.

Martin, Carter W. *The True Country: Themes in the Fiction of Flannery O'Connor*. Nashville: Vanderbilt UP, 1968.

May, John. *The Pruning Word: The Parables of Flannery O'Connor*. Notre Dame: U of Notre Dame P, 1976.

McFarland, Dorothy Tuck. *Flannery O'Connor*. New York: Ungar, 1976.

McMullen, Joanne Halleran. *Writing Against God: Language as Message in the Literature of Flannery O'Connor*. Macon, GA: Mercer UP, 1996.

Morrison, Toni. *Sula*. 1973. New York: Plume, 1982.

O'Connor, Flannery. *The Complete Stories*. New York: Farrar, 1971.

———. *The Habit of Being: Letters of Flannery O'Connor*. Ed. Sally Fitzgerald. New York: Farrar, 1979.

———. *Mystery and Manners: Occasional Prose*. Ed. Sally and Robert Fitzgerald. New York: Farrar, 1961.

Paulson, Suzanne Morrow. *Flannery O'Connor: A Study of the Short Fiction*. Twayne's Studies in Short Fiction Series 2. Boston: Twayne, 1988.

Prown, Katherine Hemple. *Revising Flannery O'Connor: Southern Literary Culture and the Problem of Female Authorship*. Charlottesville: UP of Virginia, 2001.

Rustin, Margaret and Michael Rustin. *Narratives of Love and Loss: Studies in Modern Children's Fiction*. London: Verso, 1987.

Schloss, Carol. *Flannery O'Connor's Dark Comedies: The Limits of Inference*. Southern Literary Studies Series. Baton Rouge: Louisiana State UP, 1980.

Schweickart, Patrocinio P. "Toward a Feminist Theory of Reading." *Gender and Reading: Essays on Readers, Texts, and Contexts*. Ed. Elizabeth A. Flynn and Schweickart. Baltimore: Johns Hopkins UP, 1986. 31–62.

Walters, Dorothy. *Flannery O'Connor*. Twayne United States Author Series 216. New York: Twayne, 1973.

Westling, Louise. *Sacred Groves and Ravaged Gardens: The Fiction of Eudora Welty, Carson McCullers, and Flannery O'Connor*. Athens: U of Georgia P, 1985.

Williams, Joan. "In Defense of Caroline Compson." *Critical Essays on William Faulkner: The Compson Family*. Ed. Arthur F. Kinney. Boston: G.K. Hall, 1982. 402–07.

Wood, Ralph C. "Flannery O'Connor, Martin Heidegger, and Modern Nihilism: A Reading of 'Good Country People.'" *Flannery O'Connor Bulletin* 21 (1992): 100–18.

Yaeger, Patricia Smith. "The Woman without Any Bones: Anti-Angel Aggression in *Wise Blood*." *New Essays on* Wise Blood. Ed. Michael Kreyling. Cambridge: Cambridge UP, 1995. 91–116.

How Sacred Is the Violence in "A View of the Woods"?

MARSHALL BRUCE GENTRY

Although Flannery O'Connor's "A View of the Woods" was selected for both *The Best American Short Stories of 1958* and *Prize Stories 1959: The O. Henry Awards* after originally being published in *Partisan Review*, many readers have been troubled by this story, in part perhaps because it has seemed to be reducible to an Agrarian lecture insisting on the value of southern provincialism, in part because it allows a father who abuses his child to triumph, and in part because the story seemed to be telling us things we do not want to hear about the value of a child's cooperating with her father's beatings so that she could be made a martyr for Agrarianism of a particularly Catholic sort. I once accepted the common reading that the story's violence is linked to the sacred in that the grandfather, Mr. Fortune—as he watches his son-in-law Mr. Pitts beat Mary Fortune Pitts and then later as he is finally attacked by this granddaughter—has a chance to discover the mysterious power of the woods, which have a value more religious than capitalistic.

My desire in reconsidering this story has been to find a way to like the story better. I used to think that O'Connor was intentionally putting into this story some of her less pleasant beliefs about the need to spank children regularly. I have since begun to wonder how much O'Connor approved of the extreme obedience required of her when she attended her first elementary Catholic school in Savannah (Cash 13–14). I have also wondered how O'Connor would react to charges that the Church has ignored priests' acts of child sexual abuse. I have now, I hope, reached what I consider a more satisfying point in my ongoing attempts to understand "A View of the Woods" because I see O'Connor herself standing in questioning awe about the point to which some of her principles lead her. It is as if O'Connor is asking herself whether revelations about the sacred ever come at too high a price.

While I am pleased to see Jon Lance Bacon say that O'Connor considered the cultural battle to save an Agrarian way of life to be over and lost when she wrote this story in the middle 1950s (128–29), the book most responsible for giving me a new way to consider "A View of the Woods" is a 1980 study of German child-rearing, which was a best-seller in Germany for almost two years, translated as *For Your Own Good: Hidden Cruelty in Child-Rearing and the Roots of Violence*, by the German psychologist Alice Miller. The most memorable line from Miller's book is the statement that "60 percent of German terrorists in recent years have been the children of Protestant ministers" (65). Miller explains this shocking statistic by analyzing traditional German child-rearing theories, which generally insist that a child must respect the parent to the point of voicing no real objection to any parental demand. We do not want to get carried away here with all the details of Miller's argument about the childhoods of a female teenage drug addict, of Adolf Hitler, and of a man who murders young boys, but I do want to say that I think O'Connor, at least in "A View of the Woods," intuited much of what Miller later attempted to demonstrate. O'Connor, who was deeply aware of the Holocaust and who worked it into the background of many of her stories, would probably agree with Miller's idea that the abused child may well be worse off psychologically than an adult inmate of a concentration camp:

> The abused inmates of a concentration camp...are inwardly free to hate their persecutors. [Children, however,] *must not* hate their father...they *cannot* hate him either, if they must fear losing his love as a result; finally, they do not even *want* to hate him, because they love him. (118)

Rereading "A View of the Woods" with what I imagine to be Alice Miller's angle of vision, I see a child caught in a double whammy that is worse than anything else faced by a child in O'Connor's works. On the one hand, Mary Fortune Pitts must idealize her father, absurdly forcing herself to believe that he is a good father because he has land and a way to see the woods, even denying that he beats her—a denial she expresses by repeating her terrifying refrain, "nobody beat me" (530). The story presents no clear evidence, by the way, that Mr. Pitts shares his daughter's fondness for a view of the woods; despite an apparent claim to the contrary by O'Connor herself, in a letter of 28 Dec. 1956 to "A"/Betty Hester (*Habit of Being* 189–90), all Mr. Pitts demonstrates is that he values pasture. While Mary Fortune's inclination to deny the beatings by her father is for many readers the most puzzling part of the story, Miller presents an interesting explanation. Miller discusses the absurd lengths to which abused children will often go to believe that they are loved by abusive parents (120), and she points out that Adolf Hitler, like many others, was able to claim that his abusive father did not beat him (259).

The other half of the double whammy is that things are no better with Mary Fortune's relationship to her grandfather. She probably realizes that he, too, wants to be told that nobody beats her. That it is totally absurd for her to deny the beatings—absurd because she knows that Mr. Fortune has watched her while she was being beaten—does not matter; the abused child knows that she must always give the parent what is desired, no matter how high the absurdities may mount. If Mr. Fortune looked at his own behavior with any care for its effects on the child he says he loves, he would see that for some time, he has regularly beaten his granddaughter, at least in the sense that he brings about the confrontations with Mr. Pitts that will cause the father to beat the child. At one point Mr. Fortune claims that Mr. Pitts beats the child "for no reason" (530), but on the next page it is clear that Mr. Fortune knows Mr. Pitts beats the child to revenge himself in response to Mr. Fortune's actions (531). Mr. Fortune can say to himself, "It was as if it were *he* that Pitts was driving down the road to beat and it was as if *he* were the one submitting to it" (531, my emphasis). However accurately this line describes the relationship between Mr. Fortune and Mr. Pitts, it also indicates how thoroughly Mr. Fortune ignores the harm done to his granddaughter. What Mr. Fortune wants from his granddaughter is a sense of his own control, and he is happy to trick her in order to bring about his awareness of his power. In a line that could have come from one of the German child-rearing books that practice what is sometimes called "poisonous pedagogy" (Miller 10), Mr. Fortune thinks, "With grown people, a road led either to heaven or hell, but with children there were always stops along the way where their attention could be turned with a trifle" (538).

Mary Fortune Pitts responds to her grandfather in ways that Alice Miller would predict. She gives him everything he wants, she makes a show of acting just the way he wants her to, and all the while she is silent about her feelings. The story regularly shows the reader that the child neglects to express agreement with Mr. Fortune's statements about progress, statements that are likely to bring the child into the middle of a conflict between the father and the grandfather. Although Mr. Fortune blindly assumes that she likes the earthmover she intently watches at the beginning of the story, it makes sense to believe that she hates the earthmover, but feels forced to allow her grandfather to maintain his illusions. She is basically desperate. While the grandfather thinks he is her ally, and while she probably has to try to force herself to believe that her father and grandfather are both lovable, the child has no allies in this story. Even her mother accuses her of causing Mr. Fortune to do things that hurt the Pitts family (534), and there is no sign that Mary Fortune Pitts's siblings are any comfort. When Mr. Fortune is trying to make up with his granddaughter at one point and we are told that she looked at the woods "as if it were a person that she preferred to him" (537), it is reasonable to see her as frightened and without alternatives; her desire for someone to talk to similarly leads her to talk silently to her own feet, the part of her that her father beats, which are "encased in heavy brown school shoes" (540). While one might agree with John Roos that Mary Fortune Pitts shows "trust" in and "hope" for her grandfather whenever she puts her wounded feet on his shoulders (168, 174), one might also take this gesture as a sign of the extent of the child's desperation.

Although O'Connor would agree, in the 28 Dec. 1956 letter to Hester, that if there is a "Christ symbol" in this story, the woods play "that role" (*Habit of Being* 190), I believe that the child's assertion of her fondness for the woods has little to do with Agrarian values or the various readings that emphasize the significance of the woods as a Christ symbol. Mary Fortune's assertions about the woods have more to do with the required allegiance to her father and her constantly failing quest for someone with whom she could be her true self. Perhaps she treats her feet and her woods as if they were people because on a couple of occasions in the story, she does at least achieve a bit of relief by allowing her feet to carry her out into the landscape.

Mr. Fortune tells himself, of course, that his granddaughter is totally independent and strong, with only one tiny bit of her that is fouled with the genes of Mr. Pitts. The truth is that she has formed her character while she is around her grandfather—not with the goal of expressing her own needs and desires, but rather with the goal of mirroring him in precisely the ways he demands. Even Mr. Fortune is able to say (without realizing what he is admitting) that when he is supposedly having a battle with his granddaughter and complimenting himself for making her independent, he is really only demonstrating the extent of the control he has over her: "He had frequent little verbal tilts with her but this was a sport like putting a mirror up in front of a rooster and watching him fight his reflection" (531). When Mr. Fortune tells her that he "refuse[s] to ride a Jezebel" in his car, he is pleased that the child's answer is "And I refuse to ride with the Whore of Babylon" (533). When he tries to continue his toying with Mary Fortune Pitts by pointing out that "A whore is a woman!" and adding "That's how much you know!" (533), it does not occur to him that her ignorance about the meaning of her own words calls into question her supposed independence. Mr. Fortune refuses to admit that Mary Fortune Pitts gives her grandfather the kind of talk he demands without an adult level of thought behind it. I agree with Margaret Earley Whitt that the child "is a pawn in a role that is larger than her comprehension" (129). Mr. Fortune and Mr. Pitts are killing the child's soul, without paying attention enough to realize that they are doing it, and this breaking of the spirit occurs long before the child is killed physically at the end of the story.

Katherine Hemple Prown makes the fascinating argument that Flannery O'Connor, early in her career, wrote to express feminist complaints against patriarchy, but that she then learned to quiet those female voices. "A View of the Woods" is an unusual story, according to Prown, because in it "O'Connor never entirely suppressed the female-sexed voice" (113). For Prown, Mary Fortune Pitts is powerful: "the narrator never subjects her to the ironic observation that she is not really the person she believes herself to be. *Her* pride, in other words, remains justified" (155). As much as I admire this approach to O'Connor, on this story I think Prown understates O'Connor's critique of patriarchy. I prefer to see O'Connor as more feminist than Prown does, to regard O'Connor's goal to be to show us how the patriarchy enjoys playing with its feminist puppets. Her father and grandfather reduce Mary Fortune Pitts into an abject child, without pride, probably without a sense of believing herself to have a self. Although I question Richard Giannone's labeling of Mary Fortune as "irksome," he is correct to emphasize "Mary Fortune's loss of…her will to paternal cruelty" (*Flannery* 209, 208).

While it may seem that Mary Fortune's acts of violence near the end of the story prove that her will has not been broken, Alice Miller suggests the opposite: "[P]eople who must always be on their guard to keep the dam that restrains their feelings from breaking," Miller claims, may "experience occasional outbursts of inexplicable rage directed against substitute objects or will resort repeatedly to violent behavior such as murder or acts of terrorism" (65). Mary Fortune's bottle-throwing episode at Tilman's store (542–43) may have less to do with her thinking that Tilman looks like a devilish snake, or with her objecting to Tilman's buying land from Mr. Fortune, than with the fact that she can substitute him for the father and grandfather toward whom she feels such strong and taboo rage. Her subsequent and climactic attack on her grandfather may also be read as an expression of forbidden rage against her father.

If we want to, of course, we may still choose to read the story as being essentially about Mr. Fortune, and certainly O'Connor's careful reworking of Mr. Fortune's final vision suggests that she may have thought of Mary Fortune Pitts at times as a prop for analyzing Mr. Fortune. I am generally inclined to interpret O'Connor's protagonists as unconsciously setting traps for themselves to reconnect with ideals they reject on the conscious level, and one can construct such a reading of Mr. Fortune. To some extent, Mr. Fortune wants to become one of the Pittses. In this reading, he identifies with Mary Fortune not merely because she is a Fortune, but more importantly because she is a Pitts and because Mr. Fortune views her as his connection to the Pitts family. Also to some extent, he values the Pittses' closeness to the land, what he perceives as their closeness to each other, their fertility (since pits are seeds, after all), and the strategy for defeating death that the Pittses' fertility implies. While consciously rejecting the Pittses, Mr. Fortune even constructs ironic tributes to them by digging literal pits all over the landscape. One could also argue that Mr. Fortune longs to be beaten by Mr. Pitts and thus be forced to submit to Mr. Pitts's values. When Mr. Fortune unconsciously plots to trick Mary Fortune Pitts into preferring her father over him, Mr. Fortune in effect admits that it is inherently more valuable to be a Pitts than to be a Fortune.

Mr. Fortune's desire for union with the Pittses comes out even in his insistence on his own purity. As soon as Mr. Fortune says he is "PURE Fortune," he sees in the child's face "the Pitts look, pure and simple," and as a result of his imagined similarity to the child, he is able, however illogically, to feel "personally stained by it, as if it had been found on his own face" (541). Mr. Fortune is perfectly capable of interpreting the child's "Pitts look" as evidence of his own contrasting purity as a Fortune; that he chooses to imagine within himself the stain of Pitts indicates a deeper, countering desire. Mr. Fortune forces himself toward Mr. Pitts finally by deciding to whip Mary Fortune in the manner used by Mr. Pitts. Mr. Fortune tells himself that by whipping Mary Fortune Pitts he will be able to improve his relationship with her, but he surely senses on some level that to attempt to whip a Pitts will bring matters to a head. When the child attacks her grandfather, it is surely significant that Mr. Fortune "seemed to see his own face coming to bite him from several sides at once" (545). When he is almost beaten, Mr. Fortune looks up "into his own image" and hears the potentially profound words, "I'm PURE Pitts" (545). I think this would be the moment when Mr. Fortune has the chance to change his life, and his actions do deliver the land to Mr. Pitts, perhaps as Mr. Fortune desired all along. Perhaps Mr. Fortune could also become another in a series of O'Connor's males for whom redemption is experienced as transformation into a female who is being raped. Is this not the experience of Tarwater, raped at the end of *The Violent Bear It Away*, and of Asbury Fox, transformed in "The Enduring Chill" into a Yeatsian Leda about to be raped by a god in the form of a bird-shaped waterstain? If one focuses one's attention on Mr. Fortune, it may be possible to accept the almost absurd interpretation that his granddaughter becomes the rapist finally delivering the seed that the name Pitts implies.

But Mr. Fortune rejects the transformation he has prepared for himself, not so much when he kills his granddaughter as when he ultimately pronounces, "There's not an ounce of Pitts in me" (545). I think Margaret Earley Whitt and Richard Giannone are absolutely correct in pointing out that when Mr. Fortune finally sees a "huge yellow monster which sat to the side, as stationary as he was, gorging itself on clay" (546), he is actually looking at his dead granddaughter in her yellow dress (Whitt 131; Giannone, *Flannery* 213). Presumably Mary Fortune's position in death is not sitting, but lying with her face in the dirt, her mouth open. Not only has Mr. Fortune made sure that his granddaughter will always be a Pitts (for she will never grow up to marry and change her name), but he has also stopped seeing her as human. Flannery O'Connor is perfectly capable of writing works in which a murder helps to bring about a murderer's redemption—one thinks of Hazel Motes's killing Solace Layfield in *Wise Blood*, or of Tarwater's killing Bishop in *The Violent Bear It Away*. But I think there is no other work by O'Connor in which the murder victim is so thoroughly robbed of a soul.

In the letter to Hester of 28 Dec. 1956, O'Connor says Mary Fortune "is saved and [Mr. Fortune] is dammed [sic] and there is no way out of it, it must be pointed out and underlined" (*Habit of Being* 190). I fear that this answer to a correspondent's question has been taken as an insistence by O'Connor that suspense about Mr. Fortune's spiritual outcome should be the reader's major concern. Whether O'Connor intended to or not, she wrote a story here in which the plight of the abused child is more emotionally affecting than the issue of whether Mr. Fortune can find a strategy for saving his own soul. I have not yet mentioned that there is talk in the story of how Mr. Fortune is accustomed to finding his granddaughter in his bed most mornings, and the removing of Mr. Pitts's belt as preparation for beating a child implies what Richard Giannone has called the father's "phallic power" ("Displacing" 83)—so we can say that at least the threat of sexual abuse also hovers over the story. I can accept Katherine Hemple Prown's bold assertion that at the story's end, the reader may even be tricked into enjoying a display of incest: "the reader is permitted the voyeuristic pleasure of watching as the death/rape scene unfolds and the old man literally mounts Mary Fortune" (52–53).

I have reviewed a lot of very good O'Connor criticism in preparing this essay, and I am struck by the variety of ingenious strategies we critics are able to construct for downplaying the horror of what is done to Mary Fortune Pitts. There is plenty of evidence that in her own life, O'Connor worked to find value in "'mysterious' suffering" (Edmondson 140), and sometimes we look for ways in which the suffering of Mary Fortune might be good for her. Sometimes we call her death an accident caused by her grandfather's love for her (Kazin 61). Sometimes we say that the beatings and the child's reactions to them are more "symbolic" than real (Wyatt 75). They are seen as fitting into Mary Fortune's plan to exercise power over her father and grandfather (Giannone, *Flannery* 209). They are seen as portions of a philosophical stance the nine-year-old child has worked out, like a belief in "the sanctity of the pastoral landscape" (Westling 170) or "a vision of family, life and nature that is beyond that of the pursuit of Lockean self-interest" (Roos 165). They are seen as part of the child's development, "in a warped way," into "a Christ figure" (Burkle 67). While I understand and appreciate such readings, I also want us to remind ourselves of the story's horrors for the "frightened child" who gets up from the dinner table to be beaten by her father (534). I want to say, as Flannery O'Connor herself taught me to, that if it's all just a symbol, then to hell with it.

I am grateful that O'Connor abandoned her original ending for the story, an ending that might be taken to be saying that Mary Fortune Pitts had to go through all of her suffering so that her father could have a climactic recognition scene. Sally Fitzgerald, as editor of *The Habit of Being*, provides the abandoned ending in a footnote:

> Pitts, by accident, found them that evening. He was walking home through the woods about sunset. The rain had stopped but the polished trees were hung with clear drops of water that turned red where the sun touched them; the air was saturated with dampness. He came on them suddenly and shied backward, his foot not a yard from where they lay. For almost a minute he stood still and then, his knees buckling, he squatted down by their sides and stared into their eyes, into the pale blue pools of rainwater that the sky had filled. (190n)

Joanne Halleran McMullen detects patterns of circularity in this story (125–26), and it is easy for me to see why they belong. I probably would not believe it if the story attempted to suggest that Mr. Pitts would learn his lesson on the basis of finding the bodies. He could probably find vindication in the scene. Before we shut down the story by deciding on its meaning, before we make all the violence a pathway to the sacred or the philosophical, let us remember that Mr. Pitts, triumphant, with a wife and six kids left, shows no sign of breaking out of the circular patterns of abuse. The story's final version asks us to wonder how Mr. Pitts will pick the next family member to suffer his fury.

WORKS CITED

Bacon, Jon Lance. *Flannery O'Connor and Cold War Culture*. Cambridge Studies in American Literature and Culture 72. New York: Cambridge UP, 1993.

Burkle, Howard. "The Child in Flannery O'Connor." *The Flannery O'Connor Bulletin* 18 (1989): 59–69.

Cash, Jean W. *Flannery O'Connor: A Life*. Knoxville: U of Tennessee P, 2002.

Edmondson, Henry T., III. *Return to Good and Evil: Flannery O'Connor's Response to Nihilism.* Lanham, MD: Lexington, 2002.

Giannone, Richard. "Displacing Gender: Flannery O'Connor's View from the Woods." *Flannery O'Connor: New Perspectives*. Ed. Sura P. Rath and Mary Neff Shaw. Athens: U of Georgia P, 1996. 73–95.

———. *Flannery O'Connor, Hermit Novelist*. Urbana: U of Illinois P, 2000.

Kazin, Alfred. Rev. of *The Complete Stories*, by Flannery O'Connor. *New York Times Book Review* 28 Nov. 1971: 1, 22. Rpt. as "Flannery O'Connor: *The Complete Stories*." *Critical Essays on Flannery O'Connor*. Critical Essays on American Literature. Ed. Melvin J. Friedman and Beverly Lyon Clark. Boston: Hall, 1985. 60–62.

McMullen, Joanne Halleran. *Writing against God: Language as Message in the Literature of Flannery O'Connor*. Macon, GA: Mercer UP, 1996.

Miller, Alice. *For Your Own Good: Hidden Cruelty in Child-Rearing and the Roots of Violence*. Trans. Hildegarde and Hunter Hannum. New York: Farrar, 1983.

O'Connor, Flannery. *Flannery O'Connor: Collected Works*. New York: Library of America, 1988.

———. *The Habit of Being: Letters of Flannery O'Connor*. Ed. Sally Fitzgerald. New York: Farrar, 1979.

Prown, Katherine Hemple. *Revising Flannery O'Connor: Southern Literary Culture and the Problem of Female Authorship*. Charlottesville: UP of Virginia, 2001.

Roos, John. "The Political in Flannery O'Connor: A Reading of 'A View of the Woods.'" *Studies in Short Fiction* 29 (1992): 161–79.

Westling, Louise. *Sacred Groves and Ravaged Gardens: The Fiction of Eudora Welty, Carson McCullers, and Flannery O'Connor*. Athens: U of Georgia P, 1985.

Whitt, Margaret Earley. *Understanding Flannery O'Connor*. *Understanding Contemporary American Literature*. Columbia: U of South Carolina P, 1995.

Wyatt, Bryan T. "The Domestic Dynamics of Flannery O'Connor: *Everything That Rises Must Converge*." *Twentieth Century Literature* 38 (1992): 66–88.

"I forgot what I done": Repressed Anger and Violent Fantasy in "A Good Man Is Hard to Find"

DAWN KEETLEY

Flannery O'Connor was notoriously clear about the meaning of "A Good Man Is Hard to Find." In *Mystery and Manners* and in several of her letters, O'Connor claimed that the heart of the story—the moment without which "I would have no story" (112)—is the grandmother's realization of her kinship with and responsibility for the Misfit. These ties of fellowship are specifically Christian, having "their roots deep in the mystery [the grandmother] has been merely prattling about"—that is, the mystery of Christ's death and resurrection (*Mystery and Manners* 112). "She has been touched," O'Connor claims in a letter, "by the Grace that comes through [the Misfit] in his particular suffering" (*Habit of Being* 389). In return, the grandmother's gesture will "grow to be a great crow-filled tree in the Misfit's heart" and will ultimately transform him into "the prophet he was meant to become" (*Mystery and Manners* 113).

O'Connor has been equally and quite flatly clear about readings of the story she will not countenance, mostly psychological interpretations. When an English professor had the misfortune to write to her to offer a reading he and his students came up with—that the second part of the story was imagined by Bailey and that he identifies with the Misfit and "plays two roles"—O'Connor was scathing in her reply: "If it were a legitimate interpretation," she wrote, "the story would be little more than a trick and its interest would be simply for abnormal psychology. I am not interested in abnormal psychology" (*Habit of Being* 437). O'Connor finds this interpretation almost literally inconceivable and she ends by writing, "My tone is not meant to be obnoxious. I am in a state of shock" (*Habit of Being* 437). For O'Connor, the mysteries and irrationalities of humans were strictly Christian mysteries and what she called the "unreasonable" workings of divine grace: they were most definitely *not* the product of the unconscious (*Mystery and Manners* 109).

Beyond explicit directives about the meaning of her fiction, O'Connor more subtly discouraged alternative interpretations by claiming they were merely academic, even meretricious. The English professor's interpretation, for instance, is a "trick of abnormal psychology," and in her letter she goes on to lament the ways in which teachers approach a story "as if it were a research problem for which any answer is believable so long as it is not obvious" (*Habit of Being* 437). "Too much interpretation," she continued, "is certainly worse than too little, and where feeling for a story is absent, theory will not supply it" (*Habit of Being* 437). O'Connor decried readers, especially those associated with academia, who approached her fiction as "a problem to be solved," a "literary specimen to be dissected" (*Mystery and Manners* 108). The obvious reading, the pleasurable reading, the correct reading, and thus the ethical reading, she argued, was her own Christian reading.

It is with this knowledge of O'Connor's convictions, which have indelibly imprinted five decades of criticism of her story, that I offer a reading of "A Good Man Is Hard to Find" that is admittedly psychological, but also ethical. Reading beyond what O'Connor deemed the "obvious" does not have to be a morally vacuous enterprise, a mere cold-hearted and pointless dissection. Moreover, much as she would deplore the fact, O'Connor's claim that her story obviously shows the grandmother's sudden acceptance of divine grace is no longer so "obvious" to increasingly secular readers. Neither is her reading so clearly a moral one. Her specific exhortation that readers of "A Good Man" "should be on the lookout for such things as the action of grace in the Grandmother's soul, and not for the dead bodies," illustrates her more general belief that in a spiritually desolate modern world, depictions of extreme violence are warranted as the only remaining experience that could precipitate salvation—and indeed O'Connor's emphasis in her fiction is on the salvific effects of violence and not the violence itself (*Mystery and Manners* 112–13). But readers who have a difficult time doing as O'Connor urged and who do look at the violence that pervades her fiction might ask themselves if the salvation of one person's soul warrants six dead bodies.[1]

This essay does not ignore the dead bodies. In fact, it offers a secular reading that attempts to explain them. Like the maligned English professor who believed that the story utterly changes when the family's car rolls over and The Misfit drives up, I argue that the last part of the story is imaginary. It is not, however, Bailey's dream, although The Misfit does to a certain extent symbolize Bailey's rage. In the end, though, we simply do not know enough about Bailey as a character for him to become the center of the story, the source of the compelling final drama. We do, however, know enough about the grandmother, from whose point of view the story has largely been told. I propose, then, to read the second part of the story as the *grandmother's* fantasy. This interpretation puts the grandmother, along with the problem of violence, in the foreground. It suggests that the character of the grandmother has a complex interior implicitly denied in almost all critical readings, readings that follow O'Connor in seeing her as a prattling and superficial hypocrite who has depth only in the final moment and only as a passive recipient of grace. Central to this new understanding of the grandmother's character is an emotion that feminists have long recognized as forbidden to women, as the domain only of the powerful, of those who can command respect—that is, anger. Since the grandmother is unable to express her anger openly, it inevitably goes underground, emerging as the imagined slaughter of her family. In short, as the grandmother's violent fantasy, the second half of "A Good Man" enacts her repressed murderous rage against her family, a rage so horrifying to her that she first displaces it onto The Misfit and his henchman and then imagines her own expiatory death.

That the final part of the story is the grandmother's fantasy is suggested by the descriptions of the landscape in the story. Some critics have noted the distinct shift in the tone and point of view of the story after Pitty Sing leaps onto Bailey's neck and the family car rolls into a gulch (see Doxey, for example). This accident happens, moreover, shortly after the grandmother has been taking "cat naps" (16). Certainly, from this point on, the scenery irremediably changes, as if the story moves from realistic description to surreal nightmare. Early on, as the family sets off on their trip, the grandmother carefully notes details of the scenery: "Stone Mountain; the blue granite that in some places came up to both sides of the highway; the brilliant red clay banks slightly streaked with purple…The trees were full of silver-white sunlight and the meanest of them sparkled" (11). These images are reiterated in subsequent pages: red pervades the descriptions of Red Sammy's establishment, and "white sunlight" bathes the Tower where they stop for lunch (16). As the grandmother leads her family down the ill-fated dirt road to the imagined plantation, they drive through "a swirl of pink dust," look down on "the blue tops of trees," and descend into red depressions (18). All color vanishes from the landscape after The Misfit appears, however: instead of white light and blue sky, there is only the refrain about an absence of sun and an absence of cloud (23, 27). And what was once evoked as red and blue and sparkling with light becomes black and menacing: "Behind them the line of woods gaped like a dark open mouth," and, one by one, all of the family members except the grandmother move toward the "dark edge" of the woods and are swallowed by its blackness (21, 23). As Claire Kahane has perceptively noted, O'Connor's landscapes are filled with "an imagery that evokes archaic fears"—landscapes that threaten to strike, devour, and penetrate (123).[2] It is, in fact, difficult to assent to readings of the story such as Carter Martin's, which argues that the final landscape of "A Good Man" reflects the grandmother's grace, objectifying beauty and returning us to an image of "the meanest trees filled with light" (136). At best there is an absence of light; at worst, the world has become dark and engulfing as realistic color gives way to cloudless skies that are not blue, suns that are colorless, and dark woods that "gape" like mouths panting to devour. The story shifts, in other words, from landscape to dreamscape. Far from the trees sparkling with light, at the end, just before grandmother dies, the narrator remarks that "[t]here was nothing around her but woods" (27).

Color does not entirely disappear from the protracted final scene of the story, though. What was at first the red and blue of the external scenery becomes projected onto characters, serving as one way in which the imagery of the early part of the story returns in the later part in distorted and fragmented ways, just as night-dreams incorporate daytime scenes. As The Misfit and his two henchmen emerge from the car, their clothes, when not black or gray, are described as blue and red—the two colors that most persistently marked the early landscape. Hiram wears a blue striped coat, the Misfit has on only blue jeans, and Bobby Lee wears a red sweatshirt (20–21). The repeated colors point to still more clear ways in which Hiram and Bobby Lee are elements of a fantasy that incorporates earlier events. For instance, Bobby Lee, consistently described as a "fat boy" in his red sweatshirt, evokes Red Sammy—a "fat man" characterized on one of his own billboards as "THE FAT BOY WITH THE HAPPY LAUGH" (20, 13, 14). Moreover, the very fact of Hiram and Bobby Lee, the strangeness of which has gone utterly unremarked by critics, repeats the otherwise largely gratuitous story Red Sammy tells the grandmother about two men who pulled up in an "old beat-up car" and charged gas they never paid for (15). The best explanation for Hiram and Bobby Lee is that they appear in the grandmother's fantasy at the prompting of this story, for while the grandmother mentions The Misfit's escape from the penitentiary twice, she never refers to any traveling companions.

Recognizing how the final scene of the story reiterates scenes and events encountered by the grandmother earlier in the day gives a kind of unity to the story that some critics have noted is lacking. The story is unified, however, not only by what the grandmother sees and hears, but also by her desires. The grandmother's desires have been mentioned by critics mostly only to be belittled: she is a willful woman who simply wants to explore a sentimentalized version of her own past—dragging her family to visit "connections" in Tennessee, telling stories of old times and old suitors, and insisting on visiting a plantation she thinks she visited when she was a "young lady" (16). But beneath her superficial nostalgia for "better times," the grandmother displays an abiding fascination with death. The story opens, after all, with her warning Bailey that a trip to Florida could result in the death of all of them at the hands of The Misfit. The grandmother smuggles Pitty Sing into the car because she vividly imagines his death from asphyxiation if left at home (10), and a mere two paragraphs later she imagines herself "dead on the highway" (11). Early in the trip, they pass a large cotton field and the grandmother notices the "five or six graves fenced in the middle of it" and remarks on them to her grandchildren, asserting that it is a *family* burial ground (12, my emphasis). Her story about her former suitor and the watermelon ends with her pointing out that "he had died only a few years ago" (13). Considering all the references to death, it seems no accident when the narrator mentions that the grandmother wakes up from a nap just outside of Toomsboro (16). It should come as no surprise, therefore, that a woman with such a fatal preoccupation should fantasize that her entire family is killed. Indeed, such an occurrence is exactly what she *consciously* envisions in the very first paragraph—and intimations of the destruction of her family are never far from her mind.

If the story's violent ending is the incarnation of the grandmother's obsession with death, it is in part a product of her recognizing her son's potential violence. Bailey rarely speaks, and his response to his mother's stream of conversation alternates between formidable silence and angry outbursts. The first three times she speaks to him, he ignores her completely (9, 11, 14), and the first time he says anything at all it is an emphatic "No," in response to the suggestion that he drive to the plantation (17). After he reluctantly relents and adds that this is the only time he will stop, his communication with his family ends. In the direct aftermath of the accident—the inception of the grandmother's fantasy—she admits to herself for the first time that she fears his anger, so much so that she hopes she is injured "so that Bailey's wrath would not come down on her all at once" (19). Because it would be too threatening to represent to herself directly her own son's aggression, the grandmother displaces her awareness onto The Misfit, a man who believes that there is "No pleasure but meanness" (28). While The Misfit enacts this philosophy with an exaggerated éclat, it is a philosophy less spectacularly, but nonetheless steadfastly, adhered to by Bailey, whose own profound meanness can be recognized consciously by the grandmother only in grossly understated ways: "Her son, Bailey, didn't like to arrive at a motel with a cat" (10); "He didn't have a naturally sunny disposition like she did and trips made him nervous" (14); and "She knew that Bailey would not be willing to lose any time looking at an old house" (16). Beneath these banal remarks about Bailey lurks the grandmother's unconscious knowledge that in his silent contempt and absolute detachment lays a repressed violence.

In the very first paragraph of the story, Bailey is associated with The Misfit and, in this instance at least, specifically linked with the danger he poses: the grandmother says quite clearly that Bailey would be largely responsible for their deaths if he took his family into the path of The Misfit (9). While most critics have merely remarked in passing on the irony of this opening, it is more than a neat trick of foreshadowing: it dramatizes the grandmother's unacknowledged dread of her son, of his propensity to lead them all to their demise. After the accident, Bailey and The Misfit are relentlessly aligned, although this alignment is produced by a woman who needs at the same time to obscure it. The Misfit, for instance, repeats the very few things Bailey says during the car journey. His correcting the grandmother when she says the car rolled over three times—"'Oncet,' he corrected"—repeats Bailey's "This is the one and only time" when he is urged to go look for the plantation (21, 17). The Misfit's twice-stated "nervousness" about the children as they shout obnoxiously, and his request that they be kept away from him, evoke Bailey's only interaction with his children, when he too insists they shut up, as if he cannot bear their presence (21, 22, 17). The identities of The Misfit and Bailey are confused, moreover, as the grandmother talks to one and the other answers, or as she calls one while looking at the other. For example, when she names The Misfit and Bailey "said something to [her] that shocked even the children," it is The Misfit who "reddened" (22). Later on, she tells The Misfit that he is "a good man at heart," and, while such a comment would be anathema to The Misfit, it is Bailey who tells her to be quiet (23).

Bailey's death is a significant moment that dramatizes how, in the grandmother's mind, The Misfit is a displaced embodiment of Bailey's violence. As Bailey is led off to the "dark edge" of the woods to be shot, he promises, "I'll be back in a minute, Mamma, wait on me!" (23). While he does not, of course, come back, The Misfit remains—all the more clearly a dreamlike incarnation of Bailey since the latter is now gone from the story. In the unconscious logic of the grandmother's fantasy, Bailey's death signifies her heightened consciousness that Bailey *is* The Misfit—and, indeed, they are more explicitly linked after Bailey is shot. Just after Bailey is taken away, for example, the grandmother calls his name, "but she found she was looking at The Misfit squatting on the ground in front of her" (24). Bailey and The Misfit are connected at this moment not only by the grandmother's seeming to confuse The Misfit with her son, but also by the fact that a page earlier it was Bailey who was "squatting" on the ground (23). The Misfit then puts on Bailey's shirt and shortly thereafter the grandmother again calls her son's name—"Bailey Boy, Bailey Boy!"—while looking at The Misfit (26, 28). The final revelation of Bailey and The Misfit's shared identity is the climactic scene when the grandmother reaches out to The Misfit and murmurs "Why you're one of my babies. You're one of my own children!" (29). Although some critics have suggested that at this point the grandmother "goes crazy and mistakenly believes that The Misfit is her resurrected son," most read it as O'Connor intended: the grandmother has a revelation of her Christian fellowship with The Misfit, a spiritual epiphany that signals her awakening to grace (Khawaja 61).[3] I want to suggest that we read this moment literally, although without doubting the grandmother's sanity. She really does recognize The Misfit as Bailey, fleetingly seeing through the misdirections and disguises she has generated to conceal from herself her son's aggression and her fear of him. When she first sees The Misfit, the grandmother "had the peculiar feeling that the bespectacled man was someone she knew. His face was as familiar to her as if she had known him all her life but she could not recall who he was" (21). Her sense of a certain intimacy with The Misfit is repeated when he puts on Bailey's shirt: "The grandmother couldn't name what the shirt reminded her of" (26). What the grandmother cannot recall or name is her son. She does, however, move closer to doing so from one instance to the other—the inability to name suggesting that she may dimly remember what she at first could not recall at all. Her naming The Misfit her son, when she calls him her baby and her child, culminates in a movement toward dim awareness. The fact that The Misfit then shoots her, that she imagines her own death, manifests her unbearable horror as she momentarily admits to herself that Bailey's violence is perhaps most especially directed at his mother.[4]

While The Misfit represents in part the grandmother's fear of Bailey's violence, he nevertheless mostly represents the *grandmother's* aggression. The destruction of her son and his family is, after all, *her* fantasy, even though it does incorporate her repressed apprehension of her son's rage. Moreover, the fantasy closes a story that has been, from the beginning to end, about the *grandmother's* preoccupation with death.[5] Typical readings of the story tend to ignore the grandmother once The Misfit arrives on the scene, and while her character is flattened, he is consistently described in inflated terms: he has been seen as reminiscent of Oedipus, Job, Christ, Hamlet, Milton's Satan, Dostoevsky's Raskolnikov, Calvin, and Pascal. He has been seen as a "scholar" who grasps reality as it is, as an existentialist philosopher, as universal man, as prelapsarian man, as an agent of divine wrath, and as an exemplar of divine chastening.[6] My reading challenges the importance of this weighty lineage of tortured men, insisting that the story stays with and continues to develop the grandmother's character, continues to develop, more specifically, her hostility toward her family and her concomitant drive to punish herself for that prohibited and unbearable anger. It bears repeating, in support of this interpretation, that the grandmother is, at the literal level of the story, solely responsible for the accident that leads the family to their doom. She brings them down the fateful dirt road in search of a non-existent plantation; she brings the cat that leaps on Bailey's neck and causes him to lose control of the car; and she names The Misfit when to do so ensures that he will kill them. Her fatal naming of him, moreover, merely recapitulates her earlier references; from the beginning of the story to the end, she seems to call him into being by her absorption in the possibility of his presence.[7]

Feminist theorists have, since at least the 1970s, pointed out that anger is forbidden to women—that anger is, as Linda Grasso puts it in a recent book on literary representations of women's anger, "the sole prerogative of white men in power" (14). The forthright expression of anger demands not only that one have power in the world but, more fundamentally, that one is a person with rights that command respect. Feminist philosopher Marilyn Frye has argued that anger is inextricable from what she calls "domain" and from respect: "Anger implies a claim to domain—a claim that one is a being whose purposes and activities require and create a web of objects, spaces, attitudes and interests that is worthy of respect" (87). To get angry, in other words, is to make "claims upon respect" (Frye 90). The grandmother in "A Good Man," who signally has no domain that anyone respects—no purpose, no activities, no spaces, no interests, not even any memories—is, not surprisingly, utterly unable to articulate a forthright anger at the contempt she receives, and at her own complete powerlessness. Being able to express righteous anger, as feminist activists and thinkers alike have insisted, sows the seeds of revolution; through it, women can win liberation, rights, and personhood (see Kaplow and Lourde). Repressed anger, on the other hand, destroys and corrodes. Turned inward, it can become guilt and depression, or it can erupt in murderous hatred and violence (Grasso 11–14). For the grandmother, who has repressed her anger so deeply she can, without irony, think to herself that she has a "naturally sunny disposition," her anger turns into a fantasy of violence against the family who denies her respect and disallows her personhood. But even her displaced anger is so unthinkable to her, to her self-definition as "lady," that she must also imagine her own death as punishment for it.

To reorient interpretations of O'Connor's story around the psychological depth and darkness of the grandmother's character is to confront the consistency with which critics have simplified her. For most, she is hypocritical and superficial, either until the very end or until the moment she experiences grace. Stephen Bandy excoriates the grandmother for her banality—her manipulations, opportunism, insincerity, and "petty acts of deception," ending with the claim that she has "neither values nor morals" (113–14). Interestingly, he sees the grandmother and The Misfit, finally, as "mirror images"—although he makes the significant distinction that the Misfit has "struggled" to achieve his philosophical position (implying that he has read Camus and holds a principled existentialist view of the world), while the grandmother arrives at her pervasive disbelief "by accident": she just doesn't think (116). For the few critics who believe that O'Connor created a more complex interior life for her protagonist—who see, as Frederick Asals does, for instance, the second part of the story as a stripping away of her pretensions and the emergence of a more "deeply authentic self" (*Imagination* 147)—that self is inevitably described as maternal. Asals says that when the grandmother is finally bereft of her "self serving assurances," she responds to The Misfit "as a 'grand-mother' [...who] 'reach[es]' out to the need of this surrogate child" (*Imagination* 147). Another critic has called her, in this final moment, "an understanding archetypal mother figure" (Khawaja 61). Thus the grandmother is either a flat, banal character or, through the violence of external forces, she is at the last minute infused with grace or transformed into an essential mother figure. What these interpretations miss is the grandmother's internal force, the fact that she has an interior life, an unconscious life. They miss her obsession with death and, most importantly, how that obsession is also a desire. They miss how, at an unconscious level, the grandmother wants not only the deaths of her family members but also, in retribution for those very transgressive wishes, her own death.

Following a tradition of literary representations of women's anger, the grandmother's repressed rage is expressed only indirectly, manifest only in fantasy and by means of projection: her anger, that is, is carried—is externalized—by others. Most obviously, The Misfit serves as the grandmother's double, doing the biggest part of the dirty work of her unconscious desires. However, Pitty Sing, too, serves as a manifestation of the grandmother's repressed anger. In this, O'Connor's story resonates in significant ways with Edgar Allan Poe's "The Black Cat"—another southern gothic tale that is all about repressed and displaced familicidal anger.[8] Pitty Sing not only evokes Poe's cat, but recapitulates the ways in which Pluto enacts the narrator's inveterate homicidal tendencies toward a family member. The grandmother insists that she take her cat along on the family's trip, just as the black cat was inseparable from Poe's narrator, thus marking the indelibility of the desires both cats represent: "It was even with difficulty that I could prevent him from following me through the streets," Poe's narrator claims (224). Furthermore, O'Connor describes Pitty Sing as very carefully secreted—*in* a basket, *under* some newspaper, which was *under* a valise—which suggests the unconsciousness of her desires (10, my emphasis). The most crucial of Pitty Sing's actions, the leap onto Bailey's neck that causes the accident, repeats Pluto's culminating action in Poe's story—his leap between the narrator and his wife on the cellar steps—which precipitates the narrator's fatal ax blow. That the killing in "The Black Cat" is, in fact, no accident is marked by the narrator's immediately remarking: "[t]his hideous *murder accomplished*, I set myself forthwith, and with entire deliberation, to the task of concealing the body" (228, my emphasis). The narrator's language of madness abruptly disappears and he now makes repeated references to resolution, deliberation, and determination, letting slip that the death of his wife is what he has wanted all along. In his fateful leap from the basket onto Bailey's neck, Pitty Sing repeats this function of Pluto as repository of repressed hostility. Indeed, O'Connor describes Pitty Sing's jump with words that insinuate involuntary rather than conscious action. As J. Peter Dyson has noted, Pitty Sing is released by "a series of reactions in which the parts of [the grandmother's] body and her suitcase take on an identity and life of their own… and act out, independently, the meaning and consequences of the perception she has just had: 'Her eyes dilated…her feet jumped up…the valise moved, the newspaper top…rose with a snarl,' climaxing in 'and Pitty Sing, the cat, sprang'" (155). Like Pluto's apparently random leap and the narrator's unplanned and "mad" blow with the ax, Pitty Sing and the grandmother seem to move without purpose or volition. In both cases, however, seemingly unintentional action manifests the hostile directives of the unconscious.

Dyson is the only critic to have written in a sustained way about how Pitty Sing functions as the grandmother's double, but while he claims that the cat expresses "a dimension of her self of which she is largely unaware," he then goes on to argue that the cat acts out the grandmother's willfulness (153–54, 155, 156). My disagreement with this reading lies in the fact that, as Dyson himself points out, willfulness is perhaps the predominant character trait of the grandmother throughout the story; it has been evident from the beginning. Therefore, to see the cat as enacting that willfulness adds no depth to the grandmother's character. The discussion of Pitty Sing as the grandmother's double is thus rendered rather futile, for the cat embodies no trait that is not *already* immediately apparent. However, by interpreting the cat's concealed presence in the car and deadly leap onto Bailey's shoulder as the manifestation of the grandmother's repressed rage at her family, something new is revealed—something intimated, although not already fully explained, by the grandmother's earlier preoccupation with death.

A final reference to Poe's story illuminates the way in which O'Connor's story asks us to read the ending precisely as the revelation of something as yet unread within the grandmother. The early description of Pitty Sing lying concealed in a basket under "a big valise that looked like the head of a hippopotamus" (10) evokes Poe's narrator's discovery of the seemingly reincarnated Pluto in a bar: "my attention was suddenly drawn to some black object, reposing upon the head of one of the immense hogsheads of gin, or rum" (226). I am tempted to suggest that O'Connor consciously refers to Poe here and in her cat concealed beneath a hippopotamus's head playfully inverts his image of a cat perched on top of a hogshead. More particularly, O'Connor's placement of Pitty Sing under the hippopotamus's head rather than standing on top of a hogshead hints rather dryly at the obvious way in which the second part of Poe's story, after the narrator kills Pluto but suddenly discovers him again in the bar, is the narrator's rather flagrantly purposeful "delusion." The obviousness of the narrator's hatred of his wife is signaled by Pluto's being clearly visible on *top* of the hogshead. O'Connor, on the other hand, by having Pitty Sing thoroughly concealed, suggests that the grandmother's wishes are less obvious, less a barely-concealed conscious wish than a desire she cannot admit to herself.

Poe's "The Black Cat," however, is as much about the narrator's compulsion to be caught and punished as it is about his desire to commit murder. Similarly, O'Connor's story is about the grandmother's desire to be punished—punished for a murderous rage she cannot admit. Strangely, though, and again like Poe's story, the grandmother's desire for punishment seems devoid of any sense of right or wrong; she seems free of any *indwelling* conscience. Indeed, it is The Misfit onto whom the grandmother projects her need for punishment—just as she projects onto him her forbidden anger. O'Connor marks the absence of the grandmother's conscience by writing it into the story as *visibly* absent. This process begins as early as the first paragraph, when the grandmother, having told Bailey that a convict has escaped from the Federal Penitentiary and is heading for Florida, proclaims: "'I wouldn't take my children in any direction with a criminal like that aloose in it. I couldn't answer to my conscience if I did'" (9). This solitary time that conscience is named is notable for the grandmother's multiple displacements of it, even as she invokes it. One way in which conscience is displaced is that she is claiming that *she* would not take the children into danger, therefore *she* would not be troubled by her conscience; secondly, even though she is using the first person ("I couldn't answer to my conscience if I did"), she is in fact referring to Bailey ("You couldn't answer to your conscience"); and, third, the two emphatic negatives ("I wouldn't," "I couldn't"), regardless of the actual meaning of the sentences, serve to distance conscience as the object of the last sentence. Despite the grandmother's exiling of conscience here, the irony is, of course, that she *does* take the children into the path of The Misfit and she *does* have to answer for it. Her violent fantasy of her family's slaughter mandates her punishment, though since the grandmother is alienated from her anger, she is equally alienated from any understanding of why she is impelled toward self-punishment.

Such a close reading of these two early sentences is profitable because they dramatize, in small, a dynamic that pervades the first part of the story: the grandmother consistently acts without conscience while also evoking it. As virtually every critic of the story has noted, the grandmother displays less than admirable behavior as she deceives and manipulates her family to get what she wants—and she does so apparently without compunction. She brings the cat along, for instance, knowing Bailey does not want it, and feels only justification in defying her son (10). And, most egregiously, she lies to the children about the plantation house she wants to visit. She tells them there is a secret panel, causing them to screech relentlessly until their father agrees to go. She does so, "not telling the truth but wishing that she were" (17). Despite her willful blindness to her own moral lapses, the grandmother is nevertheless vigilant about those of others, exhorting her grandchildren in particular to be respectful of others—"of their native states and their parents and everything else"—and telling them they should be ashamed when they are not (12, 15). This inconsistency in the grandmother's behavior, along with the refrain about the search for the elusive "good man," suggests her longing for conscience in a world where people, including herself, signally display none. It is important, I think, that O'Connor writes that while the grandmother did not tell the truth about the secret panel, she "wish[ed] that she [did]."[9]

As Marilyn Frye has argued, anger is signally about being wronged, and in order to be wronged, "you have to be or be perceived as right. Anger is always righteous," she continues. "To be angry you have to have some sense of the rightness or propriety of your position" (86). With her anger unavailable to her, the grandmother loses the ability to make moral distinctions—to grasp what is right and wrong about herself and others. Indeed, the story as a whole laments a society that has lost the moral grounding that should be the sole basis of punishment. Instead, in "A Good Man," punishment is an end in itself. Punishment is its own justification, and to be punished is the only way a person knows he or she has done something wrong.

The grandmother's apparent lack of a conscience, while all the time chastising others, sets the stage for the appearance of her *externalized* conscience, whose need to punish has only been strengthened by its denial. While the grandmother's fantasy summarily effects her family's death (displaced of course onto The Misfit and his henchman), the same fantasy is also riven with guilt. While Bobby Lee and Hiram actually kill the family, enacting the grandmother's buried rage, it is The Misfit, in his preoccupation with crime and guilt, who embodies her need for punishment. The Misfit is obsessed with the lack of fit between crime and punishment, and in this he dramatizes precisely that repression of her anger that leaves the grandmother so helplessly vulnerable to a punitive conscience she cannot grasp.

So, while the grandmother's fantasy clearly manifests her need for punishment, even for her own death, she never acknowledges directly the source of her guilt—the nature, that is, of her "crime." As The Misfit talks about his crime and his punishment, his recurrent claim is that he does not remember the crime: "I done something wrong," he says, but upon the grandmother's asking what he did, he replies: "I forget what I done, lady. I set there and set there, trying to remember what it was I done and I ain't recalled it to this day" (25–26). Waxing more philosophical, he goes on to reflect that "You can do one thing or you can do another, kill a man or take a tire off his car, because sooner or later you're going to forget what it was you done and just be punished for it" (26–27). This refrain of his forgetting, the single salient fact about The Misfit's crime, represents the indecipherability to the grandmother of her own "crime"—of her absolute inability to own her repressed and consequently murderous anger against her family. Perhaps the only hint of a recognition of her familicidal impulses is in The Misfit's claim that doctors at the penitentiary insisted that he had killed his father (26). While he cannot remember his crime, however, The Misfit never disputes that he deserves punishment. At one point the grandmother says that maybe he was sent to the penitentiary by mistake, but he replies: "'Nome,' he said. 'It wasn't no mistake. They had the papers on me'" (26). Later, he repeats that "they could prove I had committed [a crime] because they had the papers on me" (27). In this (albeit somewhat baffled) acceptance, The Misfit also dramatizes the grandmother's uncomprehending sense that she deserves punishment, just as he then enacts that need for punishment by killing her.

The inability of The Misfit and the grandmother to remember crimes for which they nevertheless feel they need to be punished joins with the generally unconscionable behavior of everyone else in the story to create that moral wasteland which O'Connor herself and most critics see as a central theme of the story. But my reorientation of the meaning of story away from O'Connor's diagnosis of the problem as a religious one (Americans have lost their faith) suggests a different problem that is, however, no less an ethical one: people have lost an *indwelling* conscience. And in the grandmother's case, at least, the root of this loss lies in her inability to own her (righteous) anger, as she buries it along with a sense of what is right and wrong. In her blindness to the "crime" for which her (externalized) conscience punishes her, the grandmother loses any hope of understanding, expressing, and thus perhaps resolving her rage against her family.

All that seems to remain of morality in the world of O'Connor's story, where crimes are not remembered and where right and wrong lack meaning, are institutions and authorities that punish. These punitive systems operate in a world in which any understanding of the moral distinctions upon which punishment should be predicated have disappeared. Perhaps the most revelatory moment in support of this argument is when The Misfit tells the grandmother, in response to her asking why he was sent to the penitentiary: "'Turn to the right, it was a wall,' The Misfit said, looking up again at the cloudless sky. 'Turn to the left, it was a wall. Look up at the ceiling, look down at the floor. I forgot what I done lady'" (25–26). Here The Misfit recites details of the penitentiary itself when asked about the reason he was sent there. He substitutes a description of the closed confines of the disciplinary institution for any subjective grasp he might have of *why* he was there. This replacement of the punitive authority itself for an understanding of what he did wrong occurs again when The Misfit says that he knows he committed a crime "'because they had the papers on me.'" He believes this, moreover, even though "'they never shown me my papers'" (27). The only thing that marks The Misfit's morality (or immorality) to himself is an institution that punishes him. Again, the first paragraph is crucial to this thematic since the grandmother remarks in it that "'The Misfit is aloose from the Federal Pen and headed toward Florida'" (9). The Misfit has been loosed from the disciplinary institution that substituted itself for his own moral sense, that placed itself as the only indicator of The Misfit's crimes. Not surprisingly, once released from this authority, The Misfit is able to make no moral distinctions and is able to recall none of his crimes. The Misfit's moral problem is also, however, the grandmother's. And his being "aloose" from the Federal Penitentiary anticipates how she will similarly be freed into the realm of fantasy.

Like The Misfit, the grandmother's punishment is the only marker that she has indeed committed a "crime." For the grandmother, however, the institution represented by The Misfit's entrapping penitentiary is family and home—the realm she cannot leave and that defines the parameters of her existence. Home and family precipitate her "crime"—her anger—a "crime" that, like The Misfit, she cannot remember, cannot acknowledge. It is also the crime for which she must be ruthlessly punished. Certainly, The Misfit's description of the penitentiary could describe the grandmother's entrapment in her son's house: any way she turns, all she sees are walls. The grandmother, moreover, is the only character to repeat The Misfit's refrain about the cloudless sky, suggesting how he embodies not only her sense of entrapment but also her desire to escape (27). If we recognize the ways in which the grandmother is trapped in a house full of people who despise her, some earlier parts of the story take on a greater poignancy, such as June Star's snide remark, after her brother tells his grandmother that if she doesn't want to go to Florida she should stay home: "She wouldn't stay at home to be queen for a day" (10). That the grandmother probably rarely leaves the house, and has no control over when she does and where she goes if she does, explains exactly why the grandmother wouldn't stay home. In fact, seeing Pitty Sing as the grandmother's double suggests that it may be she, not he, who would "accidentally asphyxiate" herself if she stayed home, intimating an unbearable suffocation and even suicidal thoughts. Her being first in the car, desperately anxious to leave, and her interest in writing down exactly how many miles they have gone, become the actions of a woman who cannot wait to get away and who wants a tangible marker of her escape when she is forced to return (10).

The fact that the grandmother is not only trapped, but trapped within a family that seemingly despises her, clarifies the murderous anger which her fantasy manifests and for which she so severely and blindly punishes herself. It is telling evidence of the critical propensity to read the grandmother as a flat character that while critics have often noted how cruel her family is to her, they never envision her as having any response to it. Her family members' contemptuous dismissal, disrespect, and even latent violence, along with her confinement and her inability to express her forthright anger, all seem more than adequate to explain why she may fantasize their deaths. The story suggests she has no other options. Even escape into the past is undermined as an option, since the grandmother's memories are presented as self-consuming, their emptiness figured in the watermelon that she remembers was left by a former suitor (now dead), that was inscribed E. A. T. and that was duly eaten before she got it (13). It is also figured in the plantation she seeks, which she remembers visiting as a young lady. She remembers many details about it, but then realizes with a horrifying shock that it is not there at all—a shock that directly precedes and precipitates her deadly fantasy, as the loss even of her past leaves her face-to-face with nothing but her family—their hatred of her and her own repressed aggression toward them.

In the end, then, the violence in O'Connor's story is the grandmother's fantasized response to the inhumanity and thinly disguised aggression of her family, to her entrapment, to the meaninglessness of her memories, and, above all, to her inability to express her anger about any of it. The fantasy is also, in incorporating her own death, about her self-punishing guilt for such a fantasy, for the violent emergence of her buried anger. Such an interpretation does not look for an explanation in the original sin suggested by O'Connor, neither does it look to the lack of religious faith she also insisted upon—but it is no trick of "abnormal psychology," no meaningless academic exercise. It is, rather, an ethical reading that urges us to look for problems closer to home, and *in* the home, by locating the story's violence in the family and in a patriarchal social code that forbids and renders unintelligible women's anger.

NOTES

1. This is a point made by Kathleen Ochshorn in "A Cloak of Grace." As she puts it: "that pile of dead bodies cannot be canceled out when the grandmother touches The Misfit" (114). However, Ochshorn does not go on to offer a reading that considers the implications of those bodies; she argues instead that the grandmother is not good enough for the grace O'Connor claimed she received. "Essentially, the story is a stronger indictment of the grandmother and her pathetic view of life than of The Misfit" (116). See Stephen Bandy's "'One of my babies'" for similar, though more extended argument.
2. See also Gilbert Muller's descriptions of the "menacing and alien" landscape in "A Good Man" (81–84).
3. Jefferson Humphries articulates the typical reading of this moment perfectly: "Bringing death, the Misfit brings the grandmother of "A Good Man Is Hard to Find" to a searing intuition of the sacred, out of the old-womanly selfishness which has defined her character throughout the story...She reaches such clarity of vision that she is able to recognize what she and the Misfit have in common, and to pity his hopelessness...For the instant before she dies, the sacred takes hold of this old lady and for perhaps the first time in her life she is filled with charity" (118).

4. In general, one of the most perceptive interpreters of this story, Frederick Asals has suggested that, while The Misfit "has his own reasons" for shooting the grandmother, "he also symbolically acts out the rage that Bailey has smothered, the repayment of all her crafty domineering and self-serving hypocrisy, for the smuggled cat, the dirt road, the car accident, the blurting out of the name that ensures the family's doom" (*Imagination* 153). My primary difference with Asals, aside from reading the last part of the story as the grandmother's dream, is that I recognize Bailey's culpability for his "smothered" rage. Asals seems to read it as quite understandable given the grandmother's annoying character flaws. For instance, Asals sees Bailey's sullenness and anger as a response to the grandmother's hypocrisy and manipulative behavior while I tend to see the grandmother's subterfuge as a way to deal with Bailey's absolute uncommunicativeness, contempt and smoldering rage. She is afraid to confront him.
5. In this, of course, my reading differs from the famous interpretation of the English professor and his students that so shocked O'Connor. Their reading posited that Bailey "imagines the appearance of the Misfit" and "identifies himself with the Misfit and so plays two roles in the imaginary last half of the story" (*Habit of Being* 436). While I agree that the last part of the story is "imaginary," I do not agree that the imagination that creates it is Bailey's: his character, for one thing, is simply too undeveloped to bear the weight of such a fantasy, for us to contemplate his suddenly having such a complex interior. Moreover, the reading demands that we shift our attention from the grandmother to Bailey—and the story, as I have shown, insists too much on common elements between both parts of the story—common elements that form the perceptions of the *grandmother*. She is the protagonist and the shaping consciousness from beginning to end.
6. The typical shift of readings from the grandmother to The Misfit as center has been represented as a flaw in the story by Doxey, who notes the shifting point of view after the accident and remarks that at the end we realize we know more about the Misfit than the grandmother, "whom initially we were led to accept as the main character" (97). I argue for the story's cohesiveness as I argue that in learning about The Misfit we actually learn about the grandmother. The summary of readings of The Misfit is drawn from Sloan 75–76. For a good example of an essay that focuses on The Misfit as main, even heroic, character, see Jones.
7. Asals makes the points that "the accident is not accidental at all, but the responsibility of the grandmother," and he goes on to say that, specifically, it is her "rampant selfishness, her sentimentality, gentility, nostalgia, materialism, and uncertain hold on reality" that contribute to the "accident" (*Imagination*

149–50). He pulls short of saying that the grandmother is responsible for The Misfit, however, and for the death of her family, even as the outcome of unconscious desires (150). In fact, he discusses only Bailey's rage as being symbolically enacted through The Misfit—not the grandmother's anger (153). In this, he is representative of critics who make the grandmother out to be only what she appears, with no anger and no unconscious wishes.

8. Details evocative of "The Black Cat" that are less central to the thematic connection I want to suggest between the two stories are the notable fact the narrator of Poe's story has a "small monkey," mentioned twice, just as does Red Sammy. And, finally, the "secret panel" that the grandmother makes up in the plantation house she wants to visit—where the family silver was hidden "when Sherman came through"—suggests the infamous cellar in Poe's story where the monks of the Middle Ages walled up victims (O'Connor 16–17, Poe 228).
9. In emphasizing this desire on the grandmother's part of the truth—and in taking her longing to find a good man mostly seriously, I attribute a moral depth to the grandmother that most critics ignore, seeing her as only deceitful, manipulative, and hypocritical. Again, I think she is more complex than that and displays a desire for moral value throughout, even though she does not act upon that desire. For those critics who attack the grandmother's morality, see Ochshorn and Bandy.

WORKS CITED

Asals, Frederick. *Flannery O'Connor: The Imagination of Extremity*. Athens, Georgia: U of Georgia P, 1982.

———. ed. *Flannery O'Connor: 'A Good Man Is Hard To Find.'* New Brunswick, New Jersey: Rutgers UP, 1993.

Bandy, Stephen C. "'One of my babies': The Misfit and the Grandmother." *Studies in Short Fiction* 33 (1996): 107–17.

Doxey, William S. "A Dissenting Opinion of Flannery O'Connor's 'A Good Man Is Hard to Find.'" In Asals, *Good Man* 95–102.

Dyson, J. Peter. "Cats, Crime, and Punishment: *The Mikado's* Pitti-Sing in 'A Good Man Is Hard to Find.'" In Asals, *Good Man* 139–63.

Frye, Marilyn. "A Note on Anger." *The Politics of Reality: Essays in Feminist Theory*. Freedom, California: The Crossing Press, 1983. 84–94.

Grasso, Linda M. *The Artistry of Anger: Black and White Women's Literature in America, 1820–1860*. Chapel Hill, North Carolina: U North Carolina P, 2002.

Humphries, Jefferson. "Proust, Flannery O'Connor, and the Aesthetic of Violence." *Flannery O'Connor: Modern Critical Views*. Ed. Harold Bloom. New York: Chelsea House, 1986. 111–24.

Jones, Madison. "A Good Man's Predicament." In Asals, *Good Man* 119–26.

Kahane, Claire. "Flannery O'Connor's Rage of Vision." *Critical Essays on Flannery O'Connor*. Ed. Melvin J. Friedman and Beverly Lyon Clark. Boston: G.K. Hall, 1985. 119–30.

Kaplow, Susi. "Getting Angry." *Radical Feminism*. Ed. Anne Koedt, Ellen Levine, and Anita Rapone. New York: Quadrangle Books, 1973. 36–41.

Khawaja, Mabel. "Rhetoric of Irony and Prejudice in Flannery O'Connor's 'A Good Man (Woman) Is Hard to Find.'" *Xavier Review* 15 (1995): 55–63.

Lourde, Audre. "The Uses of Anger: Women Responding to Racism." *Sister Outsider*. Freedom, California: The Crossing Press, 1984. 124–33.

Martin, Carter. "'The Meanest of Them Sparkled': Beauty and Landscape in Flannery O'Connor's Fiction." In Asals, *Good Man* 127–37.

Muller, Gilbert H. *Nightmares and Visions: Flannery O'Connor and the Catholic Grotesque*. Athens, Georgia: U of Georgia P, 1972.

Ochshorn, Kathleen. "A Cloak of Grace: Contradictions in 'A Good Man Is Hard to Find.'" *Studies in American Fiction* 18 (1990): 113–17.

O'Connor, Flannery. A *Good Man Is Hard to Find and Other Stories*. New York: Harcourt, 1955.

———. *The Habit of Being*. New York: Farrar, Straus and Giroux, 1979.

———. *Mystery and Manners*. New York: Farrar, Straus and Giroux, 1961.

Poe, Edgar Allan. "The Black Cat." *Complete Tales and Peons*. New York: Vintage, 1975. 233–30.

Sloan, Gary. "Mystery, Magic, and Malice: 'A Good Man Is Hard to Find.'" *Journal of the Short Story in English* 30 (1998): 73–83.

Misfit Bodies and Errant Gender: The Corporeal Feminism of Flannery O'Connor

NATALIE WILSON

Although Flannery O'Connor famously denied any direct links with a feminist perspective, her disclaimer that "I just never think...of qualities which are specifically feminine or masculine" (*Habit of Being* 176) reveals a certain feminist leaning—namely that gender is culturally induced and that there are no inherent "feminine qualities"—and, her fictional oeuvre often reveals a conception of corporeality as both socio-historical and material, a notion at the heart of much contemporary feminist thought. Although O'Connor herself and a whole litany of her critics have insisted on the undoubtedly religious nature of her work, her fiction also consistently focuses on the body as a radically material entity that is profoundly shaped (and constricted) by social forces. While this concentration is sometimes muted and often ambiguous in her fiction, it nevertheless seems to contradict a key tenet of her religion—that the flesh should be subordinated and denied.[1] Her stories, on the contrary, repeatedly affirm the undeniably corporeal nature of existence.

Although O'Connor sometimes stresses this materiality as evidence of our fall from grace, she just as often presents corporeality *as* our saving grace. Approaching her work from a secular perspective (something some have claimed is impossible), I find—despite her personal assertion that she was not a feminist and the claims of many theorists that her work reveals a hatred of the female body—that O'Connor's fiction speaks in a feminist, corporealized voice.

While various critics have suggested her work is aimed at upholding norms and depicts the female body as a site of limitation, I read O'Connor as critical of the norms of her culture, especially the supposed inferiority and limited capacity of the female body as maintained by her era and region.[2] Whereas her fiction undoubtedly portrays female bodies as the victims of violence and often mocks female characters, it also depicts the surrounding societal forces that lead to such violence and that entrap females in limiting, debasing social positions. In so doing, her stories—whether she admits it or not, whether she is even consciously aware of it—offer a *feminist* critique.

FEMINIST TRAITOR OR MUTED AGITATOR?: UNEARTHING POLITICAL CONTEXT IN O'CONNOR'S FICTION

Although O'Connor has often been accused of being an anti- or non-feminist, many recent studies have questioned this claim. For instance, Katherine Hemple Prown considers O'Connor's work in light of the culture in which she lived and worked, suggesting that her seeming misogyny results from her societal positioning. One of Prown's key arguments asserts that while O'Connor's early works had a feminist bent, her later published work was profoundly shaped by her attempts to be part of the masculinist literary tradition (2). Prown argues for a "gradual silencing of female-sexed voice" in O'Connor's oeuvre (2). Maintaining that O'Connor's attempts to align herself with the male literary tradition of the South led her to create "a series of narratives that are unmistakably misogynist" (160), Prown, at various points in her treatise, constructs O'Connor as a quasi-feminist traitor, she softens this blow eventually, conceding that O'Connor never completely banishes the female voice in her fiction and that a number of works actually enact a rebellious critique of male power (157).

While I agree with Prown that O'Connor's fiction often seems to mute any overt feminist intention, I would like to make a shift in focus in order to emphasize the ways in which O'Connor's sustained focus on the body reveals an inherent championing of materiality and simultaneous denunciation of societal forces that attempt to control, restrict, and define bodies. Prown also notes O'Connor's tendency to focus on the body and grants that she appears "to implicitly have understood the transgressive nature of bodies unmarked by patriarchal discourse" (46). However, in Prown's estimation, those bodies which exceed or subvert such discourse are always punished. Whilst Prown may be right in her claim that O'Connor's aesthetic depended on "fetishizing the containment, mutilation, and death of female bodies" (45), I read the intent of such an aesthetic differently. O'Connor certainly does mutilate and violate female bodies, as Prown suggests, but I would argue she does so to reveal the debilitating and inescapable forces of patriarchy rather than to uphold such forces. Moreover, her depiction of negative female characters such as overbearing mothers and conceited socialites does not necessarily point to an internalized misogyny, but can be read as serving to reveal the ways in which women as well as men pass on and enforce patriarchal discourse. Women are thus not immune to O'Connor's scathing critiques—but her negative portrayals of women and excessive acts of violence against them are often used to reveal marring social contexts that enforce and maintain their inferiority. Political contexts such as these may be muted in her stories, they may even have been muted in her own psyche, but they rear up repeatedly in her fiction, and when they do, a profound pessimism for patriarchal power and the gender and racial inequalities that it maintains is markedly discernable.

ABNORMAL BODIES ON PARADE: O'CONNOR'S CORPUS AND CORPOREAL POLITICS

One of the key ways O'Connor's fiction displays a lack of faith in patriarchal order is through its parade of eccentric and nonconformist characters. From outlaws to sluts, from young tomboys to women who never want to have children, from car thieves to rapists, from the physically disabled to the freakish, O'Connor introduces us to a fascinating array of people who are, in some cases minutely, in other cases hugely, societal misfits. By focusing on such outsiders, O'Connor's stories reveal the limiting parameters of her time and region, as well as of patriarchy in general. As Richard Giannone notes in his article "Displacing Gender: Flannery O'Connor's View From the Woods," all of O'Connor's characters "stand outside the circumference of American society's definition of acceptable women and men and children, and none want to enter it" (74). This outsider status allows her characters to question, subvert, and transgress patriarchal authority. And, significantly, this outsider status is often tied to being a *body* that patriarchy defines as inferior or abnormal.

It is hardly surprising that O'Connor is fascinated with social outsiders, for she herself, in ways, was an outsider. Afflicted with Lupus from the age of twenty-five, O'Connor had an intimate experience of bodily based otherness. But, as Jeanne Campbell Reesman notes, she "believed that being set apart from society could sometimes have positive effects on the deformed one" (46). This conviction manifests itself repeatedly in her fiction through a focus on bodies "set apart from society" due to their gender, race, disability, or refusal to follow societal rules.

This fascination with the "abnormal" body permeates O'Connor's fiction, creating a somatic textual oeuvre that interrogates the bodily-based inequalities and injustices of American (Southern) society. Her fiction challenges the averted stare of American culture's bodily pretext of normality by forcing readers to look at bodies that are deformed, ill, ravaged, and mutilated. More prosaically, it also forces readers to confront bodies that are "normal" in their morphology, but which do not abide by "normal" gender codes. In so doing, O'Connor reveals an American landscape that suffers from a corporeal cultural anxiety that translates into the oppression and dehumanization of bodies which do not ally to desired cultural norms of gender, appearance, and activity.

Of course, in O'Connor's era and region, those bodies that did not ally to the norm were, for the most part, black bodies, bodies deformed physically or mentally, or "unacceptably" gendered bodies.[3] By depicting these misfit bodies in her fiction, and suggesting the constructed nature of normal and abnormal somatic categories, O'Connor's work precedes current theories that explore the way social difference and access to power functions at the level of the body. While this may not be a readily overt project in her fiction, these inclinations ally her with corporeal feminists such as Judith Butler, Lauren Berlant, and Susan Bordo. Like them, O'Connor understands that the diseased body, the abnormal body, the ugly body, the fat body, the violated body, the wrongly gendered body can lead to transgressions of bodily boundaries, to an opening out of the body that integrates it within a social cosmology. This type of body, as her work attests, cannot be easily dismissed or transcended, but plays a crucial role in the personal, the political, and the social. Thus, while her "politics" may be more hidden than other Southern writers, her work nevertheless grapples with pressing political concerns—especially the politics of embodied identity.[4]

In particular, by making strategic use of the abnormal body and analysing the way in which misfit status is tied to particular types of bodies, O'Connor reveals the extreme normalisation of the body in twentieth-century America, and more specifically, in Southern society during the 1940s and 1950s. In effect, she names the abnormal body as a subject before its disciplinary construction as such. For, while the civil rights movement, feminism, and disability studies all worked to redefine who counted as a valued and valuable subject, at the time in which O'Connor wrote there was a much more homogeneous idea of proper subjecthood—an idea that granted a privileged (and disembodied) subjecthood mainly to the "normal" white, male, middle class body and a less privileged but equally normative subjecthood to the southern belle. Thus, her work deploys the differently-abled and freakish body as a means through which to interrogate the limiting parameters of society as well as to represent different, more expansive forms of embodied subjectivity. This impetus in her work seems to be informed by her personal distance from the social category she was expected to occupy—that of the dutiful daughter with feminine grace and charm, the southern belle who dressed impeccably and never failed to be ladylike.[5]

By occupying many of her works with such unladylike women and feminine men, as well as with freakish, disabled, and subaltern bodies of all kinds, O'Connor's fiction interpolates itself with a longstanding American tradition of using the freak to solidify a concept of what it means to be a normal American. As Rosemary Garland Thomson notes in her introduction to the anthology *Freakery: Cultural Spectacles of the Extraordinary Body,* the exhibition of freaks in nineteenth-century America "exploded into a public ritual that bonded a sundering polity together in the collective act of looking. In a turbulent era of social and material change, the spectacle of the extraordinary body…confirmed commonality, and certified national identity" (4). As Thomson further argues in *Extraordinary Bodies*: "A cluster of cultural conditions dovetailed to produce the climate in which the freak show flourished: immigration, class repositioning, and increased social stratification pressed an insecure polity to invent a corporeal other whose difference relieved the apprehensions about status" (78).

Similarly, in O'Connor's era, "a cluster of cultural conditions," such as racism, class stratification, and notions of the southern belle, produced a climate in which corporeal "others" functioned both as the *material* incarnation of otherness and the target of apprehensions regarding civil rights, class politics, and gender issues. To be *truly* American (or Southern) in early to mid-twentieth century America, one needed a certain type of body, namely, one that was white, heterosexual, and productive, one that could mesh with "liberal individualism's denial of bodily limitation and dependency" (Thomson, *Extraordinary Bodies* 101). O'Connor, due to her doubly-othered status, first as a non-traditional woman and second as a person suffering from a debilitating illness, did not have this type of body. As female and diseased, she was far removed from what critic Rachel Adams refers to as "the privileges of citizenship conferred on the anonymous white male citizen" (11–12).

Significantly, O'Connor was not an outsider to such privileges only because she was female, but, more importantly, because she was *unacceptably* so.[6] As critics such as Louise Westling reveal, O'Connor adamantly refused to play the role of the southern belle and declined to conform to cultural expectations of normal femininity. Westling notes that O'Connor would not "play the part of the Southern lady," that she "refused to be ladylike, deliberately accentuating clumsy physical traits," and that she walked "slew-footed and round-shouldered" (149, 135). Westling further comments that O'Connor "preferred to wear old jeans and loose shirts with their tails hanging out" (135) and "wore an ugly sweat shirt out of pure perversity" (49)—much like the character Hulga from "Good Country People."

O'Connor's fiction reveals her enduring contempt for socially sanctioned femininity and her resentment that she was expected to dress, walk, and act in certain ways. As Westling asserts, "Nothing could be further from the beauty and grace of the southern belle than the glasses, ugly braces, and extra pounds of O'Connor's twelve-year-old girls or the wooden legs, bad hearts, and fondness for ridiculous sweat shirts and Girl Scout shoes of her mature daughters" (146). Living in a society in which women were, like children, supposed to be seen and not heard, O'Connor (and her female characters) refused to be silenced. As Patricia Yaeger observes, "Writing in a culture that refuses women their rage and intelligence, O'Connor uses both…she throws the book at a southern world in which women are not allowed to be angry, ill-mannered, intelligent, or visionary" (199). However, O'Connor was so crafty in her critique of patriarchy and the limitations it imposed on women and others that many have read her oeuvre as glorifying and upholding patriarchy rather than condemning it. To justify this reading, critics focus particularly on the punishment and violence enacted against non-traditional women.

While it is true that O'Connor's quasi-feminist characters often suffer at the hands of a brute social order, this does not mean that O'Connor approved or, as some have suggested, felt these women needed to be punished. Rather, her works reveal the confining and warping aspects of patriarchy. In particular, her fiction explores the limiting role of southern womanhood. As Westling suggests, the often negative portraits of non-traditional female characters should not be read as revealing disdain on O'Connor's part, but rather as a form of social critique which attempts to open readers' eyes to the profound impact society has on individual opportunity. Noting that many critics have noticed the pervasiveness of "bookish daughters" and disapproving mothers, Westling further points out that few "go beyond asserting that this material has autobiographical sources" (144). Like Westling, Yaeger suggests that O'Connor's critics often focus on autobiographical, religious, or regional aspects of her fiction at the expense of a more thoroughly politicized critique, that her critics are like "sleeping readers" (189).

Critics also seem to be snoozing when it comes to assessing the effects O'Connor's illness must have had on her worldview and her fiction. Many refer to the increasing degeneration and deformation of O'Connor's body caused by Lupus; few offer lengthy analysis of how the illness may have affected her work or the aims therein. And, those theorists that mention her disease and resulting physical disfigurements usually do so only in passing. For example, Westling concedes that O'Connor made "uncomplaining use of terrible illness to focus and purify her life as a writer" (53), Gilbert Muller notes that "inevitably she transferred personal agony and suffering to her work" (2), and Robert Brinkmeyer accedes that Lupus confined her to a solitary life (169).

However, there are a few noteworthy exceptions to this tendency to mention O'Connor's illness merely in passing. For example, Prown links the repeated acts of violence against female bodies in O'Connor's fiction to her illness, noting that these depictions perhaps help her to "work through some of her personal ambivalence regarding the illness that so visibly compromises her own physical integrity" (50). Asserting that her Lupus "no doubt enhanced her experience of embodiment as a trap from which there was no escape," Prown argues that the various deaths in her fiction "offered her a means of asserting symbolic control over her own errant body" (51). Linking O'Connor's personal and longstanding experience of debilitating illness to the "desire to transcend the constraints of female embodiment" apparent in her work, Prown offers a nuanced consideration of how O'Connor's own morphology may have shaped her writing (50).

In another noteworthy exception to the tendency to overlook O'Connor's illness, William F. Monroe, in his article "Flannery O'Connor and the Celebration of Embodiment," examines the effect O'Connor's Lupus had on her work. However, unlike Prown, he asserts her illness did not lead to a desire to transcend or control the body, but rather to a continual confirmation of the body in her work. Referring to "her affirmation of the hideously ordinary, the grotesquely carnal existence of the contorted 'freaks' and fanatic 'cripples' who populate her stories," Monroe argues that "this affirmation of the body as good is all the more astounding when we consider the betrayal of Flannery's own body, her 'freakish' appearance and grotesque disability" (183). Noting that Lupus gives a "bestial, wolfish" look to the face and long term cortisone therapy would have led to such bodily factors as excessive facial hair and osteoporosis, Monroe indicates that O'Connor's own experience of living in a marred body profoundly shaped her fiction. Moreover, he argues that her affirmation of the body never waned and remained evident throughout her oeuvre, even in those stories finished shortly before her death (188).

While some theorists have suggested O'Connor's work shows a desire to transcend materiality, I would counter that her fiction pervasively topples the disembodied, transcendent, materially perfect or immune body. Instead, she gives a starring role to the undeniably physical, often abnormal body. This focus is particularly apt when considered in light of O'Connor's own material specificity. For, in spite of (or perhaps because of) her illness, O'Connor reveals the body as a site of social contestation which is open not only to pain, dismemberment, gratification and pleasure, but also to the surrounding world which both affects and is affected by physical limitations and desires. She does not employ a nihilistic relation to materiality but relies on the humorous grotesque in order to counteract a morbid or depressing view of carnality. Repeatedly informed by a conception of the body *as* grotesque, her fiction eschews the concept of the classical, closed, and isolated body in favor of a dangerously open, transgressive, and grossly physical morphology.

IT'S NOT JUST BIZARRE, IT'S POLITICAL: THE GROTESQUE IN O'CONNOR'S OEUVRE

While many critics have noted O'Connor's use of the grotesque, few examine the grotesque as a socio-political trope in her work. Reesman, an exception to this tendency, asserts that in the critical assessment of O'Connor "what has been lacking is analysis of the social function of the grotesque for female protagonists" (43). Here, Reesman indicates that critics have generally not grappled with O'Connor's use of the grotesque as a social statement or her use of the grotesque body to interrogate the politics of gender. Insisting that the grotesque in O'Connor's work "is revealed most of all as a gender issue," Reesman begins the important work of politicizing the grotesque in O'Connor's fiction (40).

Yaeger also contributes to this work, but with a change in focus to racial issues. As she notes in her article "Flannery O'Connor and the Aesthetics of Torture": "When a southerner writes in the mode of grotesque realism, the body is metaphorized in a way that expresses a character's or author's troubled relation to his or her social formation" (184). Referring to the grotesque as an "ill-mannered trope" which has the "rough energy" to shatter "old norms," Yaeger emphasizes the grotesque as an aestheticized form of social protest (185). Noting that in Southern women's writing the grotesque "foregrounds social codes that are embarrassing, damaging, invisible: codes the status quo recognizes but is interested in hiding" (184), Yaeger insists on the inherently political nature of the grotesque. Arguing that "the grotesque offers a way to move back and forth between history and the body," Yaeger's argument reveals the need to examine O'Connor's works as fictional explorations of those bodies particularly marked by a southern historicity (185).

While I find Yaeger's assessment of the southern grotesque and O'Connor's place within this literary tradition brilliant and fascinating, I disagree with her on one crucial point, namely, that O'Connor "rejects the regenerative promise of the southern grotesque" (204). On the contrary, I find O'Connor's stories repeatedly indicate the body should be celebrated and revelled in rather than denied or transcended. From O'Connor's admiration for characters who enjoy or are fascinated with the body (such as child in "A Temple of the Holy Ghost" and Parker in "Parker's Back") and her disdain for characters who attempt to abnegate or transcend the body (such as Hulga in "Good Country People" and Ruby in "A Stroke of Good Fortune"), O'Connor consistently reveals a reverence for the body and its many fascinating possibilities. Like Mikhail Bakhtin, who famously celebrates the grotesque *as* material embodiment, O'Connor suggests the body is a site that both permeates and is permeated by the socio-cultural. Moreover, in spite of her own illness, she denounces transcendent yearnings and suggests the need to come to terms with our physicality. As Monroe notes, the letters she wrote leading up to her death were suffused with humor and helped her "to maintain her courage in the face of her body's revolt against itself" (186). On a similar note, Anthony Di Renzo notes that "the same laughter that sustained O'Connor while her hip bones melted away and her body swelled from cortisone sustains her novels and short stories" (96). Thus, both Monroe and Di Renzo trace O'Connor's interest in the body back to her own bodily specificity.

Interestingly, Peter Hitchcock takes a very similar approach to the work of Bakhtin. In "The Grotesque of the Body Electric," Hitchcock chronicles Bakhtin's various illnesses, including his osteomyelitis, the bone disease that precipitated the amputation of his right leg. Hitchcock maintains that these and other bodily factors intricately inform Bakhtin's work, noting that "Bakhtin, a consummate theorist of the body, begins with the unconsummated nature of his own tissue, a body that for most of his life painfully reminded him of its fleshly imperfections" (78). Hitchcock also reminds us that Bakhtin began his work on Rabelais, his "most significant statement of the body's function in art and life" around the time his leg was amputated (80). Thus, like O'Connor, who was writing on another continent at roughly the same time, Bakhtin, perhaps due to the insistence of his body that its pain could not be transcended, repeatedly writes the body into his work. This is not to say that disease, pain, or bodily imperfections precipitate or are the necessary condition of such work, but rather, that in the cases of both O'Connor and Bakhtin, both consummate writers of the body, their own bodily specificity markedly informs their writing.[7] As Hitchcock notes, "People do not write about the body merely because their body appears in permanent revolution against them but one might take on the possibility that Bakhtin's excessive body, its grotesque order of pain, has a pertinent and permanent inscription in his theorization" (78). Likewise, O'Connor's body seems to have a "pertinent inscription" in her fiction.

Both O'Connor and Bakhtin reveal in their works that the diseased or abnormal body cannot be easily dismissed or transcended and plays a crucial role in both the personal and the social. Significantly, this revelation seems grounded in each of their experiences of living in bodies marred by illness and deformation. Furthermore, while we might expect such knowledge to lead to a championing of bodily transcendence or a damnation of the limitations of the body, neither writer enacts such a body-hating treatise. Rather, they both challenge the averted stare of culture that gasps in awe and horror at abnormal bodies. In so doing, they suggest corporeality infuses all levels of being and imagine the social as a *material* space of contestation. This focus on materiality in both O'Connor and Bakhtin is critical of any doctrine that brands the body as closed, perfectible, or inconsequential. As such, corporeality is shorn of its limiting connection to the individual body and becomes instead a collective issue in which each body is part of a wider social body—or, in Bakhtin's terms, this body "is not individualized," is "contained not in the biological individual, not in the bourgeois ego, but in the people" (19).[8]

This notion that corporeality is a uniting principle that holds out the possibility for redefining the social is evident throughout the work of Flannery O'Connor. Her characters, be they missing an arm or a leg, be they suffering from eczema or acute acne, be they hermaphrodites or clubfoots, are all placed within a social realm that is in need of a renewed collectivity. The body in her work is always indicative of and related to the social—the ailing, lonely, afflicted, tattooed, and dismembered bodies that populate her fiction are presented as part of a social tapestry, a tapestry intricately woven out of many individual bodies into a combined social collective that, in O'Connor's estimation, suffers from materialistic greed, racism, corporeal abnegation, and debilitating violence. Moreover, her characters, which are prone to acne, obesity, skin ailments, fainting and heart attacks, and which must variously endure being beaten, murdered, raped, and gored by bulls, suggest the undeniable corporeal nature of subjectivity.

In O'Connor's work, as Di Renzo argues, "Far from being an isolated, inanimate blob, the human body...is a dynamic part of the body of the world" (66). As such, O'Connor's fiction, though set in the early to mid-twentieth century, is extremely relevant today. Imagining the social as *material* space made up of many types of bodies, O'Connor's work aligns with the theoretical explorations of the body enacted by feminists such as Iris Marion Young, Rosi Braidotti, Judith Butler, Elizabeth Grosz, Rachel Adams, Lauren Berlant, and Gail Weiss. Like them, she implicitly posits the body can not and should not be transcended—that, on the contrary, an opening out of the concept of "normal embodiment" holds out the possibility for a revamped social order.

UNCONTAINED FEMALE BODIES: "THE COMFORTS OF HOME"

Referring to "Comforts of Home" as a story that "hints at the frightening power of the female body," Katherine Hemple Prown ultimately maintains that O'Connor does not celebrate the subversive power of female embodiment, but rather uses the narrative to keep it "safely contained" (47). However, while the story does indicate that patriarchal power cannot be easily transgressed, I do not see O'Connor as celebrating this fact. Rather, she reveals that patriarchy mars not only female bodies, but male bodies as well.

At the outset, the narrative introduces readers to a woman whose "daredevil charity" disrupts the order of her home (383). Mother to the selfish and narrow-minded Thomas, this woman offers Sarah Ham, whom Thomas and the outer society define as a "little slut," a place to live (383). Significantly, Sarah's surname highlights her assignation in society as a mere body (or mere meat) who, because of her supposed sexual transgressions, is no better than a pig. Thomas, the conservative and accusatory son, sees Sarah as a physical threat to the comfort of "his" home. Fittingly, he acts like an ousted child jealous for his mother's affections and seems wholly unaware that, as an adult male, perhaps he should move away (or at least be willing to share) such "comforts."

But Thomas, who struggles with echoes of his dead father's voice in his head, does not seem to abide by the masculine standards his father and the wider Southern patriarchal culture in which he lives represent—after all, he does not trust Sheriff Farebrother, the symbol of patriarchal law in the story, and he resists lording that law over his mother. But he, like Sarah, is unable to escape the expectations of patriarchy. His father's voice represents this force, telling Thomas to put his foot down and "show her who's boss" (392). Though Thomas seems to question his father's macho pronouncements, he nevertheless "writes history" for his livelihood and is thus intricately connected to the language of patriarchal power (389). In fact, we learn that "At his desk, pen in hand, none was more articulate than Thomas" (391). With phallicized pen in hand, we presume Thomas is able to write a history his macho father would have been proud of. However, when Thomas is confronted by Sarah's 'threatening' female body "terror seized his tongue" (391). She, like Thomas's mother, renders him mute and inactive.

As the story progresses, Thomas is increasingly drawn to his father's voice as well as to patriarchal law (symbolized by the sheriff) and finally decides he must take action to rid his house of the supposed female threat presented by Sarah. His plans go awry, though, and when Sarah and his mother catch Thomas attempting to frame Sarah by hiding his gun in her pocketbook, he "damned not only the girl but the entire order of the universe that made her possible" (403). Then, when Sarah lunges at him, he shoots. Hearing the sound as one "that would shatter the laughter of sluts until all shrieks were stilled and nothing was left to disturb the peace of perfect order" (403–04), the narrative reveals Thomas's unconscious aim to obliterate the threatening female body in order to uphold the order of patriarchy.

Whereas Prown reads this as an attempt by O'Connor to keep threats to patriarchal power "safely contained" (47), I see the story as exposing both the limitations and the weaknesses of an ideology which attempts to keep women "in their place" and to shape men into macho brutes. Significantly, Thomas does not succeed in killing the 'little slut' but instead shoots his mother. Hence, the threat posed by Sarah is not eliminated. Moreover, the death of the mother can be read as symbolizing the difficulty in opposing patriarchy and its values, for the mother is the character that, even more so than Sarah, questions the parameters of society. Through her refusal to label people and her attempts to rise above social gossip, the mother represents someone not tainted by the marring effects of her culture. Her death, symbolizing the danger of going against the social code of the time, might be read as indicating O'Connor's violent destruction of a character who doesn't obey societal mandates. Or, it can be read as symbolizing patriarchy as a violent, debilitating force which kills even the most benign defectors (as represented by the mother) and mutilates the psyches of its constituents (as represented by Sarah and Thomas).

At the close of the narrative, when Sheriff Farebrother enters the scene "He saw the facts as if they were already in print…Over her [the dead mother's] body, the killer and the slut were about to collapse into each other's arms" (404). Here, with caustic irony, O'Connor reveals that patriarchal law will write its own version of the story, regardless of the facts. Moreover, by focusing on minute bodily details throughout the story (such as Sarah's bowed legs, self mutilation, and history of physical abuse), O'Connor highlights the *bodily effects* of living under patriarchy. Sarah and

Thomas both seem physically distorted by their society with Sarah's body functioning as a respite of pain and shame and Thomas's as a locus of denial and socialization (as symbolized by the intense pain which grips his throat when he is unable to show his mother "who's boss"). While these two characters represent bodies warped by patriarchy, the mother, at least partially, is depicted as immune to social forces. Although she is not a wholly heroic character, she nevertheless is the most sympathetic player in this brief tale. Significantly, like other admirable O'Connor characters "she had a heavy body on which sat a thin, mysteriously gaunt and incongruous head" (384). While her small head would seem to indicate a lack of intelligence, her large body houses a sense of goodness and justice. Like many other corpulent characters, (Mrs. Pritchard and Sally Virginia in "A Circle in the Fire," the child in "A Temple of the Holy Ghost"), the mother's integrity and her hope for redemption lay within her body, not her mind. As other O'Connor stories similarly suggest, the head is a suspect part of the body, for it seems to house patriarchal law.[9] Thus, in this story, the mother's incongruously small head can be read as symbolizing her unwillingness to abide by societal codes of conduct and respectability. This unwillingness, unfortunately, results in her death.

A LIFE OF PURE MIND, A BODY DENIED: "GOOD COUNTRY PEOPLE"

Another large-bodied character who strongly suggests the danger of having a "big head" is Hulga Hopewell from "Good Country People." Hulga has a Ph.D. in philosophy and constantly relies on her intellect to analyse, weigh, and decipher the world around her. However, her body does not easily abide by her desires for material transcendence. As a child, she had her leg shot off in a hunting accident. She also suffers from very poor eyesight and a heart condition. These bodily infirmities are perhaps what have prompted her to attempt to live a life of pure mind, to bury herself in books and fill her head with philosophy.[10] However, when a bible salesman visits the family farm, she decides it is time to learn about sensual pleasures. Significantly, she plots to seduce the salesman as a mental experiment, not out of physical or emotional desire. Ultimately though, the seducer becomes the seduced.

While in the hay loft of the family barn, the bible salesman convinces Hulga to let him hold her prosthetic leg before he fiendishly absconds with it, retorting "I'll tell you another thing Hulga...you ain't so smart" (291). Physically stranded in the loft, Hulga is forced to confront her corporeality. No longer the haughty genius spouting philosophy, Hulga is forced into a realization that the body does, in fact, *matter*.[11] As for the bible salesman, symbolically named Manley Pointer, his eerie habit of collecting prosthetic body parts, including a wooden leg and a glass eye, points to patriarchal society as forcing embodied identity to give way to a view of the body as collectable object. While Hulga suffers from an inflated view of her own intellect, the bible salesman suffers from a commodified view of corporeality (particularly apt in relation to Southern history's long debates over ownership of the body). On both of these levels "Good Country People" derides abnegating conceptualizations of the body. On the one hand, intellectual transcendence is viewed as a foolish and wayward pursuit that will always fail due to the corporeal facticity of existence.[12] On the other, Manley's treatment of the body as object is mocked and derided.

On yet another level, the story also disparages the ways in which patriarchy "disables" the female body. Although Hulga stalwartly refuses to accept the role of female submissiveness or to abide by the female dress code of the South (much like O'Connor herself), the theft of her wooden leg forces her into a dependent role. Symbolic of the wider thievery of female autonomy that patriarchy enacts, the theft of Hulga's leg (and her glasses) serves to link the social mandates of society to the predatory, misguided, and smarmy antics of Manley Pointer. As a humorously tragic embodiment of the patriarchal code, Manley uses cunning and dishonesty in his pursuit of "things" (291). Travelling across the countryside, he can be read as a symbol of the pervasiveness of patriarchy for, even in this out of the way matriarchal farm, the power of a masculinist social order cannot be escaped.

THE "UNPLACED MISERY" ENGENDERED BY PATRIARCHAL POWER: "A CIRCLE IN THE FIRE"

The inability to escape the damaging effects of male power is further explored in O'Connor's "A Circle in the Fire." Like "Good Country People," "A Circle in the Fire" focuses on carnal details to suggest the body as a site of social constraint and, more specifically, as in the grips of a warping patriarchal and class stratified society. When Mrs. Cope's farm is invaded by three errant boys who wreak havoc and destruction, we learn that the head boy, Powell, has one eye that "had a slight cast to it so that his gaze seemed to be coming from two directions at once as if it had them surrounded" (179). This foreboding description foreshadows the tragedy to come while symbolically indicating the omnipresent power of the patriarchal gaze. For while these invaders are mere thirteen-year-old boys, like the bull they later release, they represent male power. Their actions (and significantly, their bodily refusal to be contained or ejected) will ultimately attempt to destroy the matriarchy of the farm.

Whilst the boys are represented as having a dangerous and animalized corporeality (they smoke, bathe in the horses' drinking water, run naked through the woods), Mrs. Cope, the matriarch of the farm, represents a prim and proper female body who misguidedly cares more about social niceties than the people who surround her. The farm, which the boys dejectedly note has "so many damn women," represents an idyllic reprieve to this innocent and ill-advised woman (186). Mrs. Cope represents a traditional southern belle, a woman with flawless manners who in conversation "always changed the subject to something cheerful" (175). Her employee, Mrs. Pritchard, serves as a stark contrast to her. While Mrs. Cope sings the praises of her supposedly blessed existence (ironically after cruelly berating a farm worker for his laziness), Mrs. Pritchard remarks that all she has to be thankful for is "four abscess teeth" (177). Here, Mrs. Cope is blind to the physical aspects of existence—she does not see the exhaustion of her farm workers or the pain of Mrs. Pritchard—rather, she focuses on niceties and empty platitudes.

Significantly, these two characters also have contrasting bodies. While Mrs. Cope is "very small and trim" and has a look of "continually being astonished," Mrs. Pritchard has a "shelf of a stomach" and is "a large woman with a small pointed face and steady, ferreting eyes" (175). These bodies, one thin and proper, the other large and outspoken, have very different views of the world. On the one hand, Mrs. Cope cares about social propriety and the proper order of things. She is reluctant to say what is truly on her mind and couches her thoughts in bland, watered down statements. On the other, Mrs. Pritchard sees things like they are and bluntly speaks her mind. She knows the boys represent trouble from the moment they arrive and, much more so than Mrs. Cope, understands Mrs. Cope's daughter, Sally Virginia, and her rebellious ways.

When the three boys arrive at the farm, Mrs. Cope naively assumes the boys have stopped by merely because they are hungry. Presenting a paltry offering of crackers and soda, she is appalled that she receives "no thank you, not no nothing" (183). The boys, with their "white penetrating stares" are far from harmless, a fact that does not escape Mrs. Pritchard or the astute Sally Virginia (179). Sally spies the goings on from her bedroom window and, after watching her fill, she sticks her head out the window "crossing her eyes and hanging her tongue out as far as possible as if she were going to vomit" (185). Here, Sally attempts to perturb the boys and, significantly, does so with recourse to a bodily act far removed from how a lady should act. The boys remain, unagitated, and merely lament "Jesus…another woman" (185). Sally, stung by this rebuttal, "dropped back from the window and stood with her back against the wall, squinting fiercely as if she had been slapped in the face and couldn't see who had done it" (185). Her reaction here is noteworthy—she does not slink away or assume the role of the sensitive, easily hurt female. Rather, she bounds downstairs and tells her mother "if I had that big boy down I'd beat the daylight out of him" (185). Mrs. Cope replies: "Ladies don't beat the daylight out of people. You keep out of their way" (185). Here, not only does Mrs. Cope instruct Sally about the proper ways of femininity, she also indicates that Sally needs to be wary and "keep out of the way" of male power. Sally is undaunted, however, and, as Mrs. Cope and Mrs. Pritchard discuss how to get rid of the boys, she confidently claims "I could handle them quicker" and grips both hands together in the action of strangulation (187).

Unphased by her mother's message that a lady cannot handle such a situation, the next morning Sally "put on a pair of overalls over her dress" and "pulled a man's old felt hat down as far as it would go on her head and was arming herself with two pistols in a decorated holster that she had fastened around her waist" (190). It seems important to note that Sally puts on the overalls *over* her dress—not *instead* of a dress. On a symbolic level, she combines male and female roles (not just adopting the masculine and obliterating the feminine). Much like the child in "A Temple of the Holy Ghost," Sally seems to desire more expansive, revamped gender roles. However, her mother will not let this untraditional femininity go unchecked and retorts:

> "Why do you have to look like an idiot?…Suppose company were to come? When are you going to grow up? What's going to become of you? I look at you and I want to cry! Sometimes you look like you might belong to Mrs. Pritchard!" (190)

In this short lecture, Mrs. Cope encapsulates societal fears regarding wayward gender. "Suppose company were to come" reveals gender roles as socially sanctioned and upheld—as something "put on" in order to "fit in." With "When are you going to grow up?" she insinuates that when children become adults, they must let go of all "errant" gender activities and attributes and act "properly" male or female. With "What's going to become of you?" she hints at the harsh punishment and ostracization Sally will suffer if she refuses to be "normal." However, she makes perhaps her most significant comment when she attempts to insult Sally by saying she looks like she could be Mrs. Pritchard's daughter. For, in this statement lurks a subversive undercurrent—could Sally be like Mrs. Pritchard? Could she adopt her shrewd perceptions and strong, hefty body that refuses to cow tow to societal norms? Doesn't Mrs. Pritchard represent an alternative, and more desirable, femininity? Of course, class issues come into play here too, and if Sally were to adopt Mrs. Pritchard's ways, we assume she would also have to forego her relatively higher position on the social ladder. But—perhaps O'Connor is suggesting this: that the more open and varied forms of femininity offered to women who do not have to live up to southern belle expectations (i.e. both women of color and women of the lower classes) are preferable to the limiting and stale notions of middle- and upper-class womanhood.

Sally seems to think so, telling her mother "Just leave me be. I ain't you" (190). Then, she heads toward the woods "as if she were stalking out an enemy" (190–91). Once there, she enacts a fantasy of empowerment that not only reveals her desire to overthrow the three boys that have invaded the farm, but also her longing to embody masculine prerogatives of power, physical prowess, and authority: "I'm going to get you one by one and beat you black and blue. Line up. LINE UP!" she says as she "waved one of the pistols at a cluster of long bare-trunked pines, four times her height" (191). Here, the pines represent the boys and, as Sally continues through the forest, "muttering and growling to herself and occasionally hitting out with one of the guns at a branch that got in her way" she stops every now and then to rebuke these male stand-ins: "Leave me be, I told you. Leave me be" (191). These actions represent an attempt to break free of the role society (and her mother) force on her. Significantly, her unladylike behaviour is symbolically aimed at the boys, and, more generally, at male power. While the pine trees represent the boys, the thorns and vines that impede her progress through the woods can be read as the patriarchal impediments that hamper her attempt to embody a more masculinized role.

When Sally hears the boys' laughter and realizes they have not already left the farm as she thought, she panics and quickly hides behind a pine tree with "the side of her face pressed into the bark" (192). Like the child in "A Temple of the Holy Ghost" who has her face mashed into a nun's crucifix, Sally's body is literally marked (and marred) by patriarchy (especially if we read the pine trees as representing the boys/male power). From her hiding place, Sally watches in fascination as the boys race and play, "the sun glinting on their long wet bodies" (192). They, unlike her, are free to roam the countryside, their bodies unfettered by societal mandates. They have a bodily liberation she does not, and it is this very freedom that allows them to destroy the female run farm (and symbolically, the female body).

When Sally eventually realizes the boys are going to set the woods on fire, she tries to run "but her legs were too heavy and she stood there, weighted down with some new unplaced misery that she had never felt before" (193). In this closing scene, Sally is literally stuck in her body, unable to escape the "weight" of patriarchy, of femininity. While O'Connor leaves the reason for her "unplaced misery" up to reader interpretation, it seems that this misery involves the realization that she will have to come to terms with societal rules and limitations—that she cannot embody the freedom the boys represent and does not want to incarnate the evil power they wield. When she finally manages to run to find her mother, Sally stares at her face anew, realizing her mother's face portrays "the face of the new misery she felt, but on her mother it looked old"—or, in other words, that her mother long ago was forced into the miserable realization of societal rules—a misery Sally now wears on her own face and body (193). While rather nihilistic endings such as these have led critics to bemoan O'Connor's representation of women as innocent or ineffectual victims, her stories do not always end on such a sombre note. For example, the outcome for Sally's fictional double, the child in "A Temple of the Holy Ghost," is far less grave. Moreover, even though "A Circle in the Fire" ends in tragedy, this does not necessarily mean O'Connor intended to berate Sally for her "errant" gender or meant to imply women are incapable of running a farm. Rather, I read the story as pointing to the unfortunate inescapability of patriarchy and the gender codes it upholds.

DECAPITATING GENDER: "A TEMPLE OF THE HOLY GHOST"

In "A Temple of the Holy Ghost," O'Connor depicts what Anthony Di Renzo refers to as a "flagrant carnality" (85). Throughout its narrative arc, the tale focuses on minute bodily details such as sweat, odor, acne, and the bodily effects of puberty. This concentration seems particularly fitting for a story that will ultimately indicate the body cannot be denied.

The tale opens with an introduction to "Temple One" and "Temple Two," young teenagers who have come to the home of the female child protagonist for a weekend visit. In the first few paragraphs, we learn that these girls are "positively ugly" in their obsessions with lipstick, mirrors, and their own bodies (236). When the child learns about their nicknames, a joke which refers to their instruction by a nun to ward off male suitors by saying "Stop sir! I am a Temple of the Holy Ghost!" (238), she is first filled with humour but quickly realizes the pleasurable possibilities of such a concept. She says to herself "I am a Temple of the Holy Ghost" and "was pleased with the phrase," feeling "as if somebody had given her a present" (238). Here, O'Connor uses this phrase in a double-edged way. First, it is used to display the girl's humorous disbelief that claiming they are "Temples of the Holy Ghost" would have any affect on male suitors—that, in effect, religious beliefs regarding the body cannot squelch sexual desire or behaviour. Second, it is used to represent the protagonist's slow realization that her body is a present—a corporeal gift to be enjoyed rather than transcended or denied.

While this salute to the body and its pleasures is an obvious theme of the story, a more subdued focus is the limitations imposed upon the body due to the 'need' to conform to traditional gender roles. This theme is revealed when the cousins ask the protagonist how she knows so much about her male neighbors, and the child imagines replying:

> "We fought in the world war together. They were under me and I saved them five times from Japanese suicide divers and Wendell said I am going to marry that kid and the other said oh no you ain't I am and I said neither of you is because I will court marshal you all before you can bat an eye." (239–40)

In this daydream, the child pictures taking part in and excelling at a traditionally masculine activity—war. But she also infuses this dream with fantasies of courtship, imagining her fellow soldiers will want to marry her. However, she turns against this traditional ending and instead imagines herself as a powerful general able to court marshal any who attempt to circumscribe her freedom. Here, her fantasies reveal a desire that goes beyond the future of lipstick and mirror posing the other two girls represent.

When the girls accompany the two neighbor boys to the fair, she continues these reveries, dreaming of being a doctor, an engineer, or a saint who becomes a martyr through decapitation. But after they return, her fantasies are put to the test. As they speak in conspirational terms about the "you-know-what" they saw at the freak tent (244), the child convinces them to tell her what they saw. Awed by their elusive descriptions of a hermaphrodite, she asks, "You mean it had two heads?" (245). Here, the child's naivete leads her to assign different heads to men and women, rather than different genitals. However, it also belies her indoctrination into a social order in which women's minds are *inferior* (and thus different) to men's. Furthermore, it significantly alludes back to her earlier fantasy of being a saint decapitated by the Romans. While Prown's reading of this story suggests that "with her head removed from her body, she will be free to avoid the pain and humiliation that female embodiment brings and will have achieved the disembodied intellectualism that eludes so many of O'Connor's women" (154), on the contrary, I read this figurative decapitation as suggesting that she sees her body, not her head, as offering a "Temple" through which to escape the limitations of her culture and society. For, in her fantasy, she goes to heaven only *after* the Romans are forced to cut off her head because they were unable to induce the lions to eat her body and her body was likewise unaffected by being burned in oil. Hence, in the vision, her body is immune. Her *head*, however, is not. Thus, in an anti-Cartesian twist, she locates her self, her life, not in her intellect, but in her morphology.

This gives her assumption that the hermaphrodite must have two heads an interesting resonance—namely, that the head is what gives a body gender. For, in order to have two genders, she assumes, the hermaphrodite must have two heads—not two bodies. In her interpretation, the head (or the intellect) is thus interpreted as housing male and female. This interpretation coincides intriguingly with recent theories of gender not as predetermined or given, but as culturally maintained and constructed.[13] Like recent feminist corporeal theory, the story seems to suggest that bodily difference is not what accounts for gender inequality but rather that ideas (or the head) are what initiate, sustain, and uphold various gender norms. Thus, when the child identifies with the hermaphrodite, she merely continues her earlier fantasies in which she is not constrained by the 'limitations' of her gender. Or, as Louise Westling nicely puts it, "the demeaning conditions of adolescent femininity can be avoided by an independence which may be freakish in the eyes of the world" (143).

While this story has been read as O'Connor's "most Catholic" story, it also is one of the strongest narrative celebrations of the body and, more particularly, of the "abnormal body" (Di Renzo 81). Revealing that O'Connor does not reject "the regenerative promise of the southern grotesque" as Patricia Yaeger argues (204), nor does she use the grotesque "to mark the body—and through it the female—as the site of physical and spiritual decay" as Prown suggests (46), this story enacts an undeniable celebration of the flesh. Seemingly drawing on her own difficulties assimilating to traditional femininity, stories such as this expose O'Connor's continued fictional attempt to reconsider what it means to be a body and, more specifically, a gendered body.

Repeatedly mocking the intellect and insisting on the undeniable nature of embodiment, O'Connor's fiction, more often than not, suggests the body as the location of possibility. For it is in the disabled body, the adolescent body, the misfit body that O'Connor situates hope. Her cross-dressing twelve-year-old girls, one-legged female philosophers, chubby female adolescents, acne faced teenagers, giant matrons, and vomiting mothers-to-be are shown in all their hideousness, but also in all their glory. These characters reveal that the body is our house in the world—one that may not always be perfect, but one that we must live in just the same. Moreover, her focus on how the body undeniably determines the roles open to one on the societal stage (be that role feminine, masculine, mother, etc.) indicates an almost Foucauldian schema in which the body is shaped into "docility" via its social and cultural surroundings.[14] Whether O'Connor turns her gaze to docile bodies that abide by society's rules about gender (such as Mrs. Cope) or to abnormal bodies who attempt to write their own bodily scripts (such as Sally Virginia), her work consistently reveals that the body cannot be extracted from the social. Prescient of much current corporeal theory, her oeuvre initiates an understanding of the dialectic between body and world, a dialectic specifically brought to the foreground in much feminist thought, and, crucially, imagines the body as a *material* location able to contest social codes and constraints.

NOTES

1. Sarah Gordon notes how the patriarchal church O'Connor subscribed to promoted "the subordination and denial of the flesh" (110). For a thorough discussion of how O'Connor's works deal with the issue of this transcendent tenet of her faith, see Anthony Di Renzo's *American Gargoyles.*
2. For example, Carol Shloss suggests that O'Connor's use of the grotesque "is aimed at upholding norms" (40–41) while Katherine Hemple Prown argues O'Connor's fiction upholds the female body as a site of limitation.
3. Although these abnormal bodies are not all female, they are, as critics such as Rachel Adams have argued, *feminized bodies* in the sense that they are posited as 'Other' to the norm.
4. On this subject, Patricia Yaeger suggests O'Connor "omits the political context" that drives much Southern fiction, especially in comparison to writers such as Zora Neale Hurston and Richard Wright (191).
5. As Sarah Gordon notes, this conception of proper femininity "maintained its hold well into the twentieth century" (108). O'Connor resisted this traditional feminine role via a refusal to dress, act, or think in ladylike ways.
6. Not only did O'Connor's illness distance her from proper femininity, but also her own personal distaste for the feminine manners, dress code, and behavior required of a southern lady. On other levels, her status as intellect, writer, and Catholic separated her from the norm.
7. However, it is worth noting that much work on the material body is authored by people whose own bodily specificities lie outside the range of the normative standards of society due to illness, disability, body size, and/or sexuality. For example, see Rosemarie Garland Thomson's *Extraordinary Bodies*, Susan Bordo's *Unbearable Weight*, and Nancy Mairs, "Carnal Acts," *Writing on the Body: Female Embodiment and Feminist Theory.*
8. This notion of a wider social body as well as of the body *as social* also informs much feminist theory. See, for example, Elizabeth Grosz's *Volatile Bodies*, Susan Bordo's *Twilight Zones*, and Gail Weiss's *Body Images.*
9. As I will discuss in more detail below, the story "A Temple of the Holy Ghost" also equates the head with patriarchal law.

10. As Anthony Di Renzo points out, Hulga's favorite philosopher, Malebranche, espoused the belief that the human mind alone is real (174).
11. For a fascinating account of the various ways bodies *matter*, see Judith Butler's *Bodies That Matter.*
12. For other O'Connor stories with a similar theme, see for example "Greenleaf," "Revelation," and "Everything That Rises Must Converge."
13. See, for example, Judith Butler's *Gender Trouble.*
14. See Michel Foucault, *Discipline and Punish* 135–69.

WORKS CITED

Adams, Rachel. "Strange Company: Women Freaks, and Others in Twentieth Century America." Diss. U of California, Santa Barbara, 1998.

Bakhtin, Mikhail. *Rabelais and His World.* Trans. Helene Iswolsky. Bloomington: Indiana UP, 1984.

Bordo, Susan. *Twilight Zones: The Hidden Life of Cultural Images from Plato to O.J.* Berkeley: U of California P, 1997.

———. *Unbearable Weight: Feminism, Western Culture, and the Body.* Berkeley: U of California P, 1993.

Brinkmeyer, Robert H., Jr. "Ascetisism and the Imaginative Vision of Flannery O'Connor." *Flannery O'Connor: New Perspectives.* Ed Sura P. Rath and Mary Neff Shaw. Athens: U of Georgia P, 1996. 169–82.

Butler, Judith. *Bodies That Matter: On the Discursive Limits of 'Sex'.* New York: Routledge, 1993.

———. *Gender Trouble: Feminism and the Subversion of Identity.* New York: Routledge, 1990.

Di Renzo, Anthony. *American Gargoyles: Flannery O'Connor and the Medieval Grotesque.* Carbondale: Southern Illinois UP, 1993.

Foucault, Michel. *Discipline and Punish: The Birth of the Prison.* Trans. Alan Sheridan. New York: Vintage, 1979.

Giannone, Richard. "Displacing Gender: Flannery O'Connor's View From the Woods." *Flannery O'Connor: New Perspectives.* Ed. Sura P. Rath and Mary Neff Shaw. Athens: U of Georgia P, 1996. 73–95.

Gordon, Sarah. "'The Crop': Limitation, Restraint, and Possibility." *Flannery O'Connor: New Perspectives*. Ed. Sura P. Rath and Mary Neff Shaw. Athens: U of Georgia P, 1996. 96–120.

Grosz, Elizabeth. *Volatile Bodies*. Bloomington: Indiana UP, 1994.

Hitchcock, Peter. "Exotopy and Feminist Critique." Bakhtin: Carnival and Other Subjects: Selected Papers from the Fifth International Bakhtin Conference, University of Manchester, July 1991. Ed. David Shepherd. Amsterdam: Rodopi, 1991. 196–209.

Mairs, Nancy. "Carnal Acts." *Writing on the Body: Female Embodiment and Feminist Theory*. Ed. Katie Conboy, Nadia Medina and Sarah Stanbury. New York: Columbia UP, 1997. 296-305.

Monroe, William F. "Flannery O'Connor and the Celebration of Embodiment." *The Good Body: Asceticism in Contemporary Culture*. Ed. Mary G. Winkler and Letha B. Cole. New Haven: Yale UP, 1994. 171–88.

Muller, Gilbert. *Nightmares and Vision: Flannery O'Connor and the Catholic Grotesque*. Athens: U of Georgia P, 1972.

O'Connor, Flannery. *The Complete Stories*. New York: The Noonday Press, 1946.

———. *The Habit of Being*. Ed. Sally Fitzgerald. New York: Farrar, Straus and Giroux, 1979.

Prown, Katherine Hemple. *Revising Flannery O'Connor: Southern Literary Culture and the Problem of Female Authorship*. Charlottesville: UP of Virginia, 2001.

Reesman, Jeanne Campbell. "Women, Language, and the Grotesque in Flannery O'Connor and Eudora Welty." *Flannery O'Connor: New Perspectives*. Ed. Sura P. Rath and Mary Neff Shaw. Athens: U of Georgia P, 1996. 38–56.

Shloss, Carol. "Extensions of the Grotesque." *Flannery O'Connor's Dark Comedies: The Limits of Inference*. Baton Rouge: Louisiana State UP, 1980. 38–57.

Thomson, Rosemarie Garland. *Extraordinary Bodies: Figuring Physical Disability in American Culture and Literature*. New York: Columbia UP, 1997.

———. Introduction. *Freakery: Cultural Spectacles of the Extraordinary Body*. New York: New York UP, 1996.

Weiss, Gail. *Body Images: Embodiment as Intercorporeality*. New York: Routledge, 1999.

Westling, Louise. *Sacred Groves and Ravaged Gardens: The Fiction of Eudora Welty, Carson McCullers, and Flannery O'Connor*. Athens: U of Georgia P, 1985.

Yaeger, Patricia. "Flannery O'Connor and the Aesthetics of Torture." *Flannery O'Connor: New Perspectives*. Ed Sura P. Rath and Mary Neff Shaw. Athens: U of Georgia P, 1996. 183–206.

Educating Hulga: Re-Writing Seduction in "Good Country People"

CHRISTINE ATKINS

In the character of Joy/Hulga in "Good Country People," Flannery O'Connor creates a strong, highly educated woman with little need for patriarchal religion or traditional culture. At thirty-two, Joy/Hulga has earned a Ph.D. in Philosophy, embraces a nihilistic worldview, and does not like things other women like such as "dogs or cats or birds or flowers or nice young men" (268).

Having created a non-traditional woman, O'Connor then proceeds to humiliate her, forcing her into a psycho-sexual assault when traveling Bible salesman Manley Pointer invites her on a walk in the country and swipes her artificial leg after kissing her. The assault leaves the otherwise articulate Hulga speechless and unsure of her reasoning skills—formerly her greatest strength. As David Havird points out, by the end of the story Hulga has been stripped of her leg and all masculine qualities; humiliated by the Bible salesman, she is fixed in a submissive position, in a "state of receptivity, [where we] leave her, a normal girl" (24).

After Hulga's violation, it becomes clear that O'Connor has entrapped her in a "rape script." As Sharon Marcus argues, rape scripts "naturalize the intrusive presence of sexual violence in women's lives and fracture their subjectivity. Rape scripts suggest that women like, desire, or deserve rape, and construct women as always already victimized" (390). Moreover, rape scripts serve to justify the rapist by envisioning him as "legitimately violent and entitled to women's sexual services" (390). The presence of the Bible salesman who assaults Hulga is naturalized in part by his mysterious and omnipotent nature. He arrives out of nowhere under the premise of selling Bibles, but the true purpose of his visit is to humiliate Hulga. Ironically, although it is Hulga who first scripts a seduction of Pointer in a daydream, that script is subverted by the Bible salesman's perverse plan to entrap her.

In O'Connor's universe, such an assault is also legitimate and redemptive within the context of Catholicism. Hulga begins as an atheist and is forced into a position where she is ready to receive the word of God. The redemptive aspect of Pointer's assault functions to justify it—Hulga's psychosexual violation is just desserts for a woman brazen enough to reject religion. As Gilbert Muller has argued, "it requires an encounter with pure evil, embodied in this case in the figure of a demonic Bible salesman Manley Pointer, to annihilate Hulga's secular dignity. Her grotesque seduction by Pointer destroys her sense of order and deprives her of her philosophic foothold" (27). The one verse from the Bible which Pointer quotes underscores the need for Hulga's violation: "He who losest his life shall find it" (272). Not until Hulga repeats this verse back during the seduction scene is it clear that Hulga's loss of her leg—her rationality and her godlessness—is imperative if she is to be saved.

Although Hulga is thirty-two when the assault takes place, the violation occurs within the context of her first sexual encounter. In this sense, O'Connor suggests that rape and violation are not only natural to the female existence but also a necessary part of the coming-of-age experience. Rape functions as a violation of the female self in its psychological and physical integrity and development, and thus becomes central to the young woman's experience. The "rape" that Hulga endures is not a literal one, but it succeeds, importantly, in fracturing her subjectivity. In "rape-prone" societies (Sanday 25), the threat of rape functions on a continuum with the event itself so that a girl/protagonist in the coming-of-age text, as in life, need not be raped, per se, to suffer the effects of rape culture in her developmental process. In Hulga's case, all of her education and philosophical beliefs are, at least momentarily, ripped from her following her violation. Without her false leg—the thing that makes Hulga different, that represents the masculine, rational way of thought she has cultivated—Hulga remains, in the end, just another normal girl, submissive and receptive to the word of God and to the "natural" order of things, as transmitted through Manley Pointer. Rape scripts in coming-of-age narratives such as "Good Country People" effectively reify fictions about women's inherent physical inferiority and desire for rape. The message becomes clear: violation intrudes upon the coming-of-age experiences for all girls, even those like Hulga who seem on the surface to depart from tradition. Along these lines, Hulga's coming-of-age experience is quite typical.

More masculine than feminine, Hulga stands in stark contrast to the other women in the story, particularly the tenant farmer's wife Mrs. Freeman's daughters, Carramae and Glynese, who serve as hyperbolized manifestations of femininity. Whereas Hulga is marked by a detached rationality and a sharp mind, Carramae and Glynese are all body. Carramae is married, pregnant and constantly vomiting, and eighteen-year-old Glynese has, among many admirers, a boyfriend who "goes to chiropractor school" and who pops her neck to remove a sty (273). Physically, Hulga eschews all traces of feminine beauty. She goes about all day in a "six-year-old skirt and a yellow sweat shirt with a faded cowboy on a horse embossed on it. She thought this was funny; Mrs. Hopewell thought it was idiotic and showed simply that she was still a child" (268). The representation of hyper-masculinity as personified in the cowboy might strike Hulga as funny simply because she herself evades any easily gendered categorization—hardly the sort of woman to be impressed by the explicit machismo the cowboy represents.

Hulga's movements are not dainty. She lumbers heavily through the rooms of the house, never hiding her resentment and annoyance at the women who surround her, particularly her mother and Mrs. Freeman. In the mornings she "stump[s] around the kitchen…glance[s] at them and [does] not speak" (267). Hulga cultivates rudeness the way other women might cultivate charm and congeniality. Mrs. Hopewell excuses her daughter's rudeness "because of the leg," (266) and also because of a heart condition that keeps Hulga close to home despite her desire to be far away from the farm. Mrs. Hopewell notes that her daughter could quiet her movements but chooses not to because she prefers ugly sounds. She stands square and rigid when provoked into conversation by her mother or Mrs. Freeman.

Hulga's refusal to embrace standards of feminine beauty and politeness makes Mrs. Hopewell wish that she could "only keep herself up a little" (267) in order to improve her physical appearance. Mrs. Hopewell draws a direct connection between Hulga's education and her physical unattractiveness. It seems her education, even more than her false leg, is what sets Hulga apart from the other women in the story. As David Havird observes, Hulga has—"intellectually at least—transformed herself into a man" (22). Through education she has attempted to separate herself from her maimed, but "nonetheless female body. Through her adoption of a masculine persona, she has made submissive her female self" (Havird 23). Education makes Hulga seem to grow "less like other people and more like herself" each year (268).

Hulga's education has led her, in part, to a philosophy of believing in nothing, and her nihilistic atheistic beliefs pose a great threat to Mrs. Hopewell. God-fearing and eternally optimistic with her cache of clichés, Mrs. Hopewell is baffled and chilled by Hulga's philosophical outbursts. One day Mrs. Hopewell is particularly disturbed when she happens upon one of Hulga's philosophy books and reads the nihilistic diatribe contained within; Hulga's philosophy is, in Mrs. Hopewell's mind, a kind of "evil" (269). The humiliation that Hulga eventually undergoes confirms that Mrs. Hopewell voices O'Connor's mutual condemnation of Hulga's atheism.

At thirty-two Hulga is not a child, but her mother likes to think of her as one in part because it is more comforting than the thought of her as "a poor stout girl in her thirties who never had never danced a step or had any normal good times" (266). Sexually speaking, Hulga *is* a girl, particularly in the sense that she has yet to have an intimate sexual experience. Perhaps Mrs. Freeman's constant chatter about her own daughters' sexual experience prompts the inexperienced Hulga to explore her sexuality by trying to seduce the Bible salesman who so timely and providentially appears at her door.

Manley Pointer, the object of Hulga's affection, first described as "a tall gaunt hatless youth" (269), wins the initially resistant Mrs. Hopewell over when she learns that in addition to being "good country people," he also suffers from a heart condition (271). Everything about Manley Pointer—his unexplained appearance, seemingly out of nowhere, his mysterious background, his psychic knowledge of Hulga's medical condition—gives him a kind of supernatural quality. When he arrives at the Hopewell farm, he claims to be from "out in the country around Willohobie, not even from a place, just from near a place" (271). His disclosure that he has a heart condition, like most aspects of his identity, also seems suspicious, particularly in light of the fact that Hulga has the same condition. The admission is in fact the one thing that prompts Mrs. Hopewell to ask him to stay for dinner. Although his visit is presumably to sell Bibles, his failure to make a sale doesn't seem to discourage him much, as though his purpose in visiting the farm never had a thing to do with selling. As Hulga's soon-to-be violator and savior, Pointer's presence is naturalized and inevitable. His coming into her life seems scripted and necessary because her rape is necessary for her maturation process.

Pointer presents himself as honest and simple, a good "Chrustian" (270). Hulga, fooled by his false representation of himself, imagines him too naive and dull to comprehend her nihilistic worldview. His innocence attracts Hulga, who decides in no uncertain terms she will seduce him after agreeing to meet him for a picnic. Hulga perceives Pointer as a true innocent blinded by his Christian faith. She imagines she can re-educate him by forcing him out of the realm of innocence and into the enlightened universe of atheism. According to Robert Brinkmeyer:

> Armed with what she sees as her penetrating vision and thoroughly rational mind, Hulga perceives herself as the potential savior of those about her...Hulga sees Manley as similar to her mother: an innocent person blinded by faith—in Manley's case a Christian vision that refuses to penetrate the real. (146)

That night after agreeing to meet Pointer, Hulga fantasizes about seducing him. In keeping with her masculine nature, Hulga plays the active agent in the fantasy, and Pointer the feminine, submissive party, the one capable of "shame" (276). Hulga has already rid herself of shame with the help of years of education, which "removed the last traces of that as a good surgeon scrapes for cancer" (281). This sense that she is incapable of shame precludes the fact that the loss of her leg—its exposure and defilement by Pointer—will in fact thrust her back into the realm of shame that preceded her education.

Hulga imagines that their picnic will segue into a walk to a storage barn in the fields, a vision which foreshadows their actual encounter, and it is there, she imagines, that "she very easily seduced him and that then, of course, she had to reckon with his remorse" (276). Again Hulga perceives Pointer as possessing feminine qualities such as sensitivity and sexual naiveté. The script of Hulga's daydream forces Manley to receive her words of nihilism which, in turn, change his life and save him: "True genius can get an idea across even to an inferior mind. She imagined that she took his remorse in hand and changed it into a deeper understanding of life" (276). The irony of Hulga's fantasy is that although she imagines how she will save Pointer by defiling him, it is her violation that will result in the kind of understanding of life she imagines he will gain.

The day of the picnic, Hulga sets off to meet Pointer with her agency and rationality still intact. She arrives at the meeting place in androgynous garb—"a pair of slacks and a dirty white shirt, and as an afterthought, she had put some Vapex on the collar of it since she did not own any perfume" (277). When she discovers that she has arrived first, her initial thought is that she may have been tricked. This foreshadows the real trickery in store for Hulga. Pointer, it turns out, has simply been hiding behind a bush. When he first appears by the side of the road to take her on the picnic, he seems an explicitly phallic representation: "he stood up, very tall, from behind a bush on the opposite embankment" (277). After some flirtatious exchange between them, Pointer kisses Hulga for the first time in her life. The kiss does not impress Hulga much, nor does it interfere with the masculine persona or rational mind she has worked so hard to cultivate:

> The kiss, which had more pressure than feeling behind it, produced that extra surge of adrenaline in the girl that enables one to carry a packed trunk out of a burning house, but in her, the power went at once to the brain. Even before he released her, her mind, clear and detached and ironic anyway, was regarding him from a great distance, with amusement but with pity. She had never been kissed before and she was pleased to discover that it was an unexceptional experience and all a matter of the mind's *control.* Some people might enjoy drain water if they were told it was vodka. (278, my emphasis)

The word "control" is imperative here. Hulga, the untraditional woman not fooled by the "stupidity" of young men, experiences her first kiss not as a young girl eager for romance, but rather as a detached and cynical observer with a clinician's eye. When the pair scamper into a loft in a nearby barn to continue their foreplay, Hulga takes note of Pointer's childlike innocence. She kisses him hungrily, trying to draw out all his breath which is "clear and sweet like a child's and the kisses were sticky like a child's" (279). O'Connor indicates that this stage of Hulga's "seduction" of Pointer leaves her faculties intact: "Her mind, throughout this, never stopped or lost itself for a second to her feelings" (279).

Pointer's pleas for Hulga to confess her love for him seem to situate him in a more submissive/feminine position. Much like a woman, he insists on an expression of love from Hulga who resists his pleas: "'You ain't said you loved me none,' he whispered finally, pulling back from her. 'You got to say that'" (279). Having scripted the seduction before it actually happens, Hulga congratulates herself because "she had seduced him without even making up her mind to try" (280). Hulga pities Pointer and continues to infantilize him:

> "You poor baby," she murmured. "It's just as well you don't understand," and she pulled him by the neck, face-down, against her. "We are all damned," she said, "but some of us have taken off our blindfolds and see that there's nothing to see. It's a kind of salvation." (280)

At this point in the seduction scene, Hulga is still very much the man and Pointer the woman, on the surface at least. The tables quickly turn, however, as Hulga is revealed to have fallen into Pointer's trap—a script which sets her up for psycho-sexual violence. Suddenly, her plan to seduce him, her script, is thwarted and his true identity revealed.

Since Hulga has already decided to do away with her virginity, the prospect of being intimate with Manley Pointer isn't what threatens her. The loss of her leg, Pointer's refusing to put it back on after taking it off, forces her to experience violation and shame. Hulga's sensitivity about her artificial leg is quite apparent: "she was as sensitive about the artificial leg as a peacock about his tail. No one ever touched it but her. She took care of it as someone else would his soul" (281). The leg becomes a trope for Hulga's sexuality and so its loss connotes, in part, a sexual violation. The leg symbolizes Hulga's difference, a difference that includes a rational, intellectual nature which foregrounds the importance of the mind over the body's fragile materiality—making Pointer's insistence that she show him where the leg joins on as a way of proving her love for him strike her as obscene.

Although she reluctantly and unwilling shows Pointer her false leg, in so doing, she acts against her best judgment. Unfortunately, without the leg, Hulga's masculine persona disappears, as does her rational, detached thought. She finds herself totally dependent on Manley. More importantly, the removal of the leg functions in the way that sexual violence does—it fractures Hulga's subjectivity. Once the leg is off, and Pointer refuses to put it back on, Hulga discovers that "her brain seemed to have stopped thinking altogether and to be about some other function that it was not very good at" (282).

O'Connor's language in this seduction scene is suggestive of sexual assault. Pointer gives Hulga a "penetrating"(281) look. His eyes look "like two steel spikes" (282). Even the objects he takes out of the valise, which he arranges like "offerings" (282) to her, speak the language of impending sexual assault: whiskey, pornography, and condoms. Pointer, as it turns out, is a fetishist, a collector of "symbolic object[s] with phallic significance that [offer] protection against fears of castration" (quoted in Havird 24). When Pointer reveals his fetishistic nature to Hulga, it becomes clear that given his particular perversions, the only assault he intends to commit is the theft of her leg: "'I've gotten a lot of interesting things,' he said. 'One time I got a woman's glass eye this way'" (283). In stealing Hulga's leg, Pointer emasculates her and reestablishes the "natural" order of things—a paradigm of male dominance and female submission.

O'Connor leaves Hulga aptly violated and shamed at the end of the story, her face "churning" (283) in the dusty sunlight of the barn. Having readied Hulga for grace with his evil actions, the Bible salesman walks away with the "embodiment of her secret self" (Brinkmeyer 147) and prepares her to receive the word of God. His violation and humiliation of her are redemptive and necessary because her rejection of religion and affirmation of masculine characteristics function to undermine the patriarchal order of things. By the end of the story, Hulga is as stupid as the young men she formerly pitied, and her plan for defiling the Bible salesman has backfired into her own defilement and violation. Perhaps more importantly, the cumulative power of years of education—a central aspect of her identity—has been shattered. All that she learned is rendered useless.

Although Mrs. Freeman has the last word in the story, declaring that the Bible salesman could never have been as "simple" (284) as he appeared, the narrative essentially ends with Hulga's humiliation in the barn. O'Connor's decision to end the narrative abruptly with Hulga's violation denies Hulga any agency or even rational response to her violation. The narrative point-of-view never enters her consciousness again, leaving the reader to contemplate the fate of a woman who rejects God and attempts to transcend feminine submission. Her violation is hardly surprising considering that many girls endure such sexual humiliation in patriarchal culture. O'Connor's text merely highlights the inevitability of such violence against women.

WORKS CITED

Brinkmeyer, Robert. *The Art and Vision of Flannery O'Connor.* Baton Rouge: Louisiana State UP, 1989.

Havird, David. "The Saving Rape: Flannery O'Connor and Patriarchal Religion." *The Mississippi Quarterly* 47.1 (1993–1994): 15–26.

Marcus, Sharon. "Fighting Bodies, Fighting Words: A Theory of Rape Prevention." *Feminists Theorize the Political.* Judith Butler and Joan W. Scott, eds. New York: Routledge, 1992. 285–403.

Muller, Gilbert H. *Flannery O'Connor and the Catholic Grotesque.* Athens: U of Georgia P, 1972.

O'Connor, Flannery. "A Good Man Is Hard to Find." *Flannery O'Connor: Collected Works.* Ed. Sally Fitzgerald. New York: Library of America, 1988.

Sanday, Peggy Reeves. *A Woman Scorned: Acquaintance Rape on Trial.* Berkeley: U of California P, 1996.

"Ignoring Unmistakable Likeness": Mark Fortune's Miss-Fortune in "A View of the Woods"

AVIS HEWITT

Mary Fortune is seventy-nine-year-old Mark Fortune's nine-year-old granddaughter and Little Miss in O'Connor's 1956 short story, "A View of the Woods." What that means for her and for him as imagined human beings, and what the story within which they configure means within the context of O'Connor's relationship to the unconscious, to the body—the writerly one, the readerly one, and the body of Christ—and to feminism—not as politics but as metaphor—are the subjects of this essay. What are we viewing in "A View of the Woods"? What is it that we see in what we see?

Old Mark Fortune spends the afternoon before his death repeatedly staring out the window of his room, attempting to understand his granddaughter's new and profound vexation with him for planning to "pave paradise" and put up a gas station outside the family front door. He attempts to understand her attachment to the scenic plot of land across the road, but he has trouble finding any value in it: "Every time he saw the same thing: woods—not a mountain, not a waterfall, not any kind of planted bush or flower, just woods...A pine trunk is a pine trunk, he said to himself" (538). And certainly, in Mark Fortune's measure of commerce, holding back from the potential establishment of a tawdry consumerist strip of retail stops likely to be named Fortune, Georgia, in order to preserve a few mundane pines when "anybody that wants to see one don't have to go far in this neighborhood" to find one would be the height of folly (538). So, too, for us as O'Connor readers: why look repeatedly at "View" when we "don't have to go far" in O'Connor stories to find our requisite share of ego-driven intractableness, the hardness of heart that leads to violence and thereby returns us to reality "at considerable cost," as O'Connor herself justifies the bloody mayhem that backdrops her stories (*Mystery and Manners* 112).

Attempting to pierce the quotidian and see reality, Mark Fortune returns that fateful afternoon to his window. This last time he is granted a true view of the woods in question. In "The Nature and Aim of Fiction" O'Connor calls this true view anagogical vision, "the kind of vision that is able to see different levels of reality in one image or one situation"; this level he needs to heed because it is the one "which ha[s] to do with the Divine life and our participation in it" (*Mystery and Manners* 72). But it is, of course, the one Mark Fortune most vehemently eschews:

> The third time he got up to look at the woods…the gaunt trunks appeared to be raised in a pool of red light that gushed from the almost hidden sun setting behind them. The old man stared for some time, as if for a prolonged instant he were caught up out of the rattle of everything that led to the future and were held there in the midst of an uncomfortable mystery that he had not apprehended before. (538)

It is this "uncomfortable mystery" upon which the story turns. What old man Fortune sees in the trees the last time he looks serves as the litmus test by which his "participation in the divine life" can be judged action by action throughout the story. What we choose to do in those moments where we are made aware that we are, and have been all along, "in the midst of an uncomfortable mystery" marks us, as it marks old Mark Fortune. The following afternoon he will be caught in a violent situation, as his granddaughter bites, claws, and pummels him into accepting a more expansive worldview. O'Connor as literary theorist believes that "the man in a violent situation reveals those qualities least dispensable in his personality, those qualities which are all he will have to take into eternity with him" (*Mystery and Manners* 114). In other words, "View" provides an opportunity to discover what makes a man—what are the "least dispensable qualities of Mark Fortune and of Pitts—and what constructs femaleness—as embodied in Mary—in one of those rare O'Connor stories where femaleness is protected, not from violence, but from the snares and impositions of "Southern-lady gender prison" in the genteel tradition, by virtue of Mary Fortune Pitts's prepubescent status.

Historically, what mainly constructs femaleness in American literature is embodiment, the metaphorical embodiment of the female as "the virgin land" and the need of men, as both Annette Kolodny and Leslie Fiedler argue effectively, to escape the domination of women. Women serve metaphorically as an analogue to the power of the land to control and consume men's lives, and that makes freedom possible only to those men who overpower, desert, or destroy the very ground under their feet. The other element of the metaphor is that men may choose to control, through violence, the power of women to abandon *them*. Notions of patriarchal pillaging of the female as both land and legacy inform "View" resonantly. To provide a rounded sense of the way in which O'Connor's "habit of being" and writerly dynamics converge in "A View of the Woods," I rely on Katherine Hemple Prown's study of the subverted feminism revealed in O'Connor's work when the published pieces are compared to their manuscript forms, a subversion likely motivated by the Fugitive Agrarian literary arbiters of O'Connor's day, an epoch during which high art meant masculinist art and female foregrounding meant an automatic relegating of one's work to the "ladyland" of magazine fiction that went without critical consideration and therefore without the possibility of canonization—yet another form of "light[ing] out for the territory" (Twain 296) and deserting, figuratively, the female, that mother-earth ground of our material being that the patriarchy has sometimes treated like dirt. Connected to that is James Mellard's reading of "View" that establishes the pervasive use of the female and the maternal in the epistemic registers of the unconscious in the story. I also rely upon Patricia Yaeger's evidence of O'Connor as a writer of the body, especially the grotesqueries of the female body as tortured terrain.

Furthermore, I want to reinforce my argument that Mary serves as somatext, that she *is* the lay of the land in the story, by revisiting an early analysis of "View," one in which Sister Bertrande Meyers argues, in one of the publications that represent the intellectual force of the Roman Catholic Church in the American mid-twentieth century, that Mary Fortune is a Moses figure, the deliverer of her people. And "her people" finally does not mean old Mark Fortune, but her immediate Pitts family of which she is the youngest member. She delivers them to the Promised Land that is the 800-acre farm where they have been allowed to tenant but which, given Fortune's tyrannical ways, they have not been allowed to possess. By construing Mary not as Moses, but as the Promised Land itself, I hope to reinscribe the validity of my reading of her as "the virgin land" in a way that confirms O'Connor's explicitly prescribed intentions. She sees her texts as leading us to "participate in the Divine life"—a Divine life that subsumes many an "uncomfortable mystery," such as the unconscious, the body, and the vexed territory of femaleness.

Finally, this essay wrestles with critics who attempt to show that O'Connor's stated intentions are thwarted by her fear of Freud and her rejection of mid-century feminism, perhaps a sensible rejection in an era when feminism as a political movement certainly could not support much weight. Some touch of critical glee seems recently to attach to demonstrating ways in which O'Connor appropriated the patriarchal authority of the church in order to have an empowered voice with which to write. It is true that the writer—either of the story or of its interpretation—needs ground on which to stand. God or Freud—we choose our territory. A prudent stance would seem to be on that territory which can encompass all the other.

Thus acknowledging my own grounding, I want to complete my opening re-view of "View" by cutting back to that climactic moment when old Mark stares into the woods, hoping momentarily to burst free of his egoism and see what Mary sees there. O'Connor has argued that a good story will have at its center "an action that is totally unexpected, yet totally believable…an action that indicates that grace has been offered" (*Mystery and Manners* 118). That action occurs in "View" just at this point. It provides "the almost imperceptible intrusions of grace" (*Mystery and Manners* 112): "He saw it [the view], in his hallucination, as if someone were wounded behind the woods and the trees were bathed in blood" (538). But before he can act on the "unpleasant vision"—that is, think a thought about its meaning and mandate—its unpleasantness is interrupted by "the presence of Pitts's pick-up truck grinding to a halt below the window" so that he can "return to his bed and shut his eyes"; yet behind the closed lids he makes a fierce effort to shut out those "hellish red trunks" rising up "in a black wood" (538).

O'Connor tells us in *The Habit of Being* that she intended the woods as a symbol of Christ, and apart from our being waylaid by any intentional fallacy, we can see in them the child's clear need to preserve access to the transcendent. But Mark Fortune turns away. He rejects the child and the transcendent, refuses to see their overarching proportions in terms of ultimate reality. He wants to make it "convenient"—a pervasive twentieth-century value—for the family to re-fuel. In planning to sell the lot right in front of the house for a gas station, he sees handiness as a main perk: "Then we won't have to go down the road to get the car filled up, just step outside the front door" (531). His troubling over the fuel tank more than the transcendent recalls Christ's opposite priorities: "man does not live by bread [or gasoline] alone." Whether re-fueling the body or that modern extension of the body, the car, we are bound up inextricably in matters of the immaterial as well as the material and "shut our eyes' against these matters at a high cost. Just how much Mark Fortune has shut out from his vision—including the land on which he stands—is what I want now to begin to recount.

Recent criticism has indeed wrestled with the gender issues in "View." In particular, Richard Giannone's "Displacing Gender: Flannery O'Connor's View from the Woods" serves as an inquiry into "the theology anchoring O'Connor's remarks on gender" and then provides a reading of "View" that "puts the gender issue in perspective" (73). Giannone, who has written extensively on "View," cites specifically the comment O'Connor makes in a letter to Betty Hester, "What you say about there being two [sexes] now brings it home to me [that] I've always believed that there were two but generally acted as if there were only one" (*Habit of Being* 136). Likening this remark to the Apostle Paul's notion in Galatians 3:27 that in the Divine life "there is no longer male or female," Giannone then argues that O'Connor's fiction is a "gender free-for-all" ("Displacing" 75), a phrase that aptly overarches his conception of it as both a gender-free zone and a world of violent tumult. He convinces himself that "O'Connor drastically dislocates our usual sexist way of seeing" (75). She manages this by making both sexes look equally bad. She offers as many manipulative mothers, insolent daughters, and cliché-ridden workers' wives as she does ego-driven and malevolent fathers, sons, uncles, hired men, Bible salesmen, and alienated existential heroes like Haze Motes and Tom T. Shiftlet. O'Connor's plot trajectory, claims Giannone, "hurls her oppressors" into an "otherworldly precinct" that enables them to "feel the ultimate portent of their inhumanity" (75). Both sexes are equally flawed, and furthermore, "divine intervention" corrects human perception and yields a restorative grace that is "[f]reely and universally given" and "disarranges the roles assigned by gender and age so as to overturn the power wielded by these differences" (75). That could be, but such a reading does not take into account a "this-worldly precinct," a place where flaws and portents of inhumanity are frequently "written on the body"—a specifically female body.

O'CONNOR'S VEXED POSITION IN THE CANON

First published in the fall issue of *Partisan Review* in 1957 and anthologized in *Best American Short Stories of 1958*, "View" was a mid-century hit for O'Connor, an author who has proved herself a "greatest hit," who has been named in Daniel Burt's *Literary 100* as one of the best authors of all time, a status she shares with only two other American women writers. Categorizing her by that means, as a woman writer, rather than noting that she shares the list with Dante and Tolstoy—both of whom made the top ten—and with Dostoyevsky as explicitly Christian writers, does indeed depart from O'Connor's stated instructions for reading her work. For forty years critics have felt generally constrained to interpret her fiction according to her own theoretical dictates. In fact, James Mellard has noticed that O'Connor is one of the modern authors who has been the most successful at having her way with critics by "simply telling the critical readers how they must interpret [her] works" (625).

Until quite recently, O'Connor seems for the most part to have been exempted from all traces of authorial and intentional fallacies. Her testimony in "The Fiction Writer and His Country" that for her "the meaning of life is centered in our Redemption by Christ" and that what she sees in the world she "see[s] in its relation to that" (*Mystery and Manners* 32) has caused critics to circumvent significant landmarks on the rich terrain of her texts. Out of respect for her genius, critics who rally to her explicitly-stated Christian perspective have taken her, in the main, at her word, and critics who are put off by it frequently feel compelled to use an ostensibly oppositional theoretical lens to demonstrate O'Connor's error of faith—or to prove that other theoretical lenses betray just as clear a picture of reality as one centered on Redemption.

Mellard's bracing Lacanian interpretation of "View," argues that using Lacan's imaginary and symbolic epistemic registers and the exchanges they negotiate discursively to read the "subject" position or "self" or "ego" of the story's main characters yields an authority of the unconscious that equals the authority of theology as an interpretive premise. He finds that both God and the unconscious represent adequate forms of the Other in O'Connor's fiction, and he quotes O'Connor in reviews and letters indicating a fear of Freud's theories. That she saw Freud as a formidable "enemy" to her orthodoxy satisfies Mellard's need to challenge what he considers our long-standing willingness to be intimidated by O'Connor's voice as critic, the one stating her intentions for our reading of her texts. He triumphantly concludes that a Lacanian analysis of "View" "can provide us a means to let O'Connor have her own way. But that "way" will survive only in a displaced form that is "compatible if not specifically with her theology, then at least with postmodernist philosophy" (643). We are left cliffhanging. Can we postmoderns accommodate a win-win situation for both O'Connor's genius and her faith?

Patricia Yaeger sports a similar hermeneutics of suspicion. The experience of O'Connor's prescriptive tenets leaves Yaeger sitting "numbed at the keyboard, or if not entirely numbed, then blank, battered, joyless, and mute" as she asks, "What hysterico-political messages are being recoded in O'Connor's fictions?" (186). Yaeger determines that for years she has "been asleep when teaching and reading O'Connor's stories and novels" and that an awakening to the "personal and political terrors of her texts" opens us to "a phenomenology of pain," a "literary sadism" that passes "as an inchoate form of readerly torture" and causes us to reject her Catholicism as "the pivotal focus for her grotesques" (187). O'Connor, in her turn, rejected the lolling fascination of Americans north of the Mason-Dixon with the myriad grotesques that her fiction so freely supplies: "I have found that anything that comes out of the South is going to be called grotesque by the Northern reader, unless it is grotesque, in which case it is going to be called realistic" (*Mystery and Manners* 40).

But Yaeger is not persuaded by O'Connor's wit and, like Mellard, is wary of its prescriptive edge. She insists that O'Connor stands as the "pinnacle, the acme, the sine qua non of the grotesque in southern literary experience" as she deliberately feeds the North's "obsession with the idiots, half-wits, deaf-mutes, sideshow freaks, one-armed bandits, unruly women, conmen, old children, and angry African Americans who populate her fiction" (185). O'Connor's move, hidden perhaps from even her own view, belies an intuitive, tacit understanding that "the body is metaphorized in a way that expresses a character's or author's troubled relation to his or her social formation" (184). And the social formations of Southern culture enact a species of torture, a gnarling of each new generation as it is bent into grotesque shapes by a forced learning of hatred, shame, fear, and cruelty deemed inherent in constructions of a racist South. Lillian Smith's *Killers of the Dream* depicts her own childhood in the South as being "put into a rigid frame too intricate, too twisting" to be endured (29).

If the Southerner's spirit is rendered grotesque as it forms, then that misshapen interiority becomes written on the body. O'Connor's somatography explodes the julep-and-magnolia veneer of the genteel tradition of Dixie to expose its riddled, plundered, shrieking, agonized underside. The punishments she renders her characters—both before we meet them and on the stage of their stories—remind us that embodiment opens us to both intense pleasures and intense pains. Yaeger argues successfully that O'Connor "attacks her own characters and deliberately violates or eviscerates their political referents, the narrative coordinates that might help us make sense of her cruelty," leaving us to contemplate her fiction with "a primitive sadism that most critics convert into an old and comfortable theology" (191). And we can use that.

Katherine Hemple Prown works meticulously with the way in which O'Connor's relationship to a patriarchal ideal at the center of her theology informs the patriarchal "real" at the center of mid-century American literary life. Prown believes that O'Connor "accepted the view that art rested on male prerogative"—a view the Fugitive Agrarians were pleased to have go unchallenged—and that she was "acutely uncomfortable with her own desire to usurp that privilege" (3). In part, she dealt with her guilty ambitions by associating the gift of genuine art with "a gender-neutral God" (3) and saw, furthermore, that the work of creating art "is a good deal more than a masculine drive—it is, in part, the accurate naming of the things of God" (*Habit of Being* 126). O'Connor's artful dodges between masculine drives and prerogatives, on the one hand, and a gender-free (-for-all) naming, on the other, is the story Prown has excavated. By looking at the transactions of the Vanderbilt Southern Agrarians as literary arbiters of the mid-century when John Crowe Ransom edited the *Kenyon Review* (1939–59) and Allen Tate edited the *Sewanee Review* (1944–46) and Robert Penn Warren and Cleanth Brooks co-edited the *Southern Review* (1935–42), Prown demonstrates dramatically that their system of patronage willingly helped women writers that seemed in need of encouragement or guidance but did not accept women as peers or colleagues; moreover, getting female-authored works published was not the main hurdle. Becoming a part of the canon meant—and still means—getting reviews and critical commentary. In all of these areas, the statistics on providing publishing space and attention to women reveals alarming gender inequities.

Prown finds clear evidence that O'Connor saw "writing like a man" as her best bet for serious consideration in a male-ordered literary milieu. She learned this lesson doubly—from both Andrew Lytle, a member of the Southern Agrarian group who instructed O'Connor at the Iowa Writers Workshop during her second and formative year in graduate school, and from Caroline Gordon, a literary mentor whose modest successes as a token women in the Agrarian group seem now as much based on her two marriages to Allen Tate as on her own accomplishments as a writer. Prown concludes that comparing the unpublished manuscripts of her work with the "earlier, female-sexed voice that governed her fictional landscape and that gradually disappeared as she strove to redirect the narrative emphasis" (7) indicates that O'Connor revised at least in part to subvert her satirical wit away from males, to move males into central positions, and then to let women receive the scornful and grotesque portrayals. This choice advantaged her in additional ways: making her women grotesque broke her apart from the "ladylike" Southern writers whom the Agrarians found beneath their critical notice and gave her an outlet for the rage that percolated under her outward show of perfect genteel conformity as a young dependent Southern woman. Prown finds this duality of identities even in O'Connor's very names: in the role of the dutiful daughter she was "Mary Flannery"; as the subversive author simply "Flannery"—with the former creating a "protected space" for the latter, "the bold and unladylike writer whose work threatened to upset the social order into which she had been born" (Prown 16) if her readers began to see themselves for the grotesques that inwardly they were—and we all generally are. By sporting a double consciousness, similar to that which W. E. B. DuBois saw as necessary for African Americans to navigate successfully our cultural life, O'Connor was able to write "like a man" in terms of exercising a powerful voice and finding the critical community willing to credence it, but complex negotiations in terms of the grotesqueries of the body seem a part of the bargain she made.

THE LAY OF THE LAND AS THE RAPE OF THE EARTH

"A View of the Woods" opens with an adverbial phrase, "[t]he week before," setting readers up to wonder, "The week before what?" Eventually we learn the answer to be "the week before" the deaths of the two main characters. We first see the two in a scene about seeing; that is, Mark Fortune and Mary Fortune Pitts, his young double and apprentice, are engaged in the activity of watching. Every morning that week they have come to the construction site of "the new lakeside on one of the lots that the old man had sold somebody who was going to put up a fishing club" (525). Starting at around ten in the morning, they watch—sometimes for hours—as an earthmoving machine "systematically ate a square red hole in what had once been a cow pasture" (525). To "eat into," rather than dig up, the farmland gives a sense of wholeness aggressively cut—as with teeth. The earth as pastoral generally yields its fruits. Rather than eating into it, we take into ourselves what it bears. The immediate sense of the action here is transgressive. Framed in the gaze of it, Mary is "the child [who] did not have eyes for anything but the machine" (525). The transgressive eating mesmerizes her: "She sat on the hood, looking down into the red pit, watching the big disembodied gullet gorge itself on the clay, then, with the sound of a deep sustained nausea and a slow mechanical revulsion, turn and spit it up" (525).

Two elements of this image disturb our everyday construction-site complacency. First, the gullet "eats" to no end; it can bite off but not take in, not swallow along to the body that which ingestion would nourish. The "disembodied" have no body to receive sustenance, no body to sustain. Second, the first observation is a lie. What we are told is "disembodied" proves more embodied than we had supposed; at least, it has a stomach, the site of bodily nausea, since it emits a sound indicative of deep digestive disturbance, deeply disturbing enough to incite a round of vomiting. *Revulsion* in its Latin root means "to tear back." This rounded scene argues a tearing away at the earth by biting, by gnawing into it and then rejecting it, rather than incorporating it once consumed. Needless to say, this action serves as an analogue to the story as a whole. Mary Fortune Pitts is that lovely Georgia clay that the maw of Mark Fortune's ego consumes and then spits up.

Not only does the opening scene of the story indicate that an ecological reading of "A View of the Woods" is possible, but also that O'Connor had extensive literary precedence for enacting such tropes. The land as female is one of our oldest metaphorical assumptions and the symbolic values of Mother Earth myriad. Annette Kolodny's *The Lay of the Land: Metaphor as Experience and History in American Life and Letters* (1975) casts American ground as a particularly potent cultural symbol. Arguing that while other civilizations have undoubtedly undergone the process of invading and ravishing the pastoral paradise that was their virgin soil, the American civilization is able to hold the entire process in its four hundred years of cultural memory, "giving Americans the unique ability to see themselves as the willful exploiters of the very land that had once promised an escape" (8). Kolodny finds that inevitably "the success of settlement depended on the ability to master the land, transforming the virgin territory into something else—a farm, a village, a road, a canal, a mine, a factory, a city, and finally, an urban nation" (7).

Yet writers from William Byrd to F. Scott Fitzgerald have seen the land as the body of a woman. In 1728, Byrd described the Blue Ridge Mountains in *Histories of the Dividing Line* as a fusing of the topographical and the anatomical—with "a Single Mountain, very much resembling a Woman's breast and with other elements of the horizon taking the form of "a Maiden's Breast" (214). In 1827, almost exactly a century after Byrd, James Fenimore Cooper shapes Natty Bumppo's perceptions of the newcomer's encounter with the new land in such a way that only by an act of will can readers avoid seeing the encounter as the seduction of a female body. He writes that those who exploit the prairie are "led by the phantoms of hope and ambitious of sudden affluence, [to] the mines of the virgin territory" (3). Along with mining, these pathfinders assert themselves in such a way that "unexplored regions [are] laid open," but then those "who first penetrated the wilds" must move "deeper into the land" (2–3). Repeated linguistic emphasis on the "piercing" and "entering into" that create a sense of sexual aggression or engagement permeate the text. In 1925, almost exactly a century after Cooper, F. Scott Fitzgerald describes the continent in the concluding pages of *The Great Gatsby* as "the fresh green breast of the new world" (189). The imagery of the land as female, as a sexualized rich and ripe body to be conquered and claimed, experienced and exploited, persists as an overarching theme of much of American literature. Its intrigues pervade our cultural life to the point of including the pre-pubescent. Although Mary Fortune Pitts fails to generate an immediate comparison to Jon Benet Ramsey, the sexualizing of the innocent and relatively androgynous bodies of children serves to remind us of forces we leave unnamed in order to leave unleashed. Sexualized land holds a man in place, perhaps even against his will. The urge that opposes stasis, even stasis that empowers the conqueror by granting him domain, is the urge to flee. Owning land, possessing a woman—these twin triumphs imply settling down. How can one insure continued dominion where one does not dwell? In old Mark Fortune's case, the instinct is ever toward mobility—bringing the paved road nearer his land, bringing the gas station nearer the house in order to keep the cars on the road. The June 1956 signing of the Interstate Highway System into law under Dwight Eisenhower dramatically altered the American sense of place, made seemingly limitless the limits of our ranging, our notions of accessibility.

The value we assigned rootedness plummeted further. That Flannery O'Connor was that summer of 1956 writing "View," a story in which an old man lusts after forms of "progress" that inhere in the automobile, seems no coincidence.

Much has been made of the hegemonic male figure in our literature as one who must periodically "light out for the Territory," as Huck does in the concluding moments of his *Adventures.* And Fiedler further postulates in his classic work, *Love and Death in the American Novel* (1960) that the civilized and domesticated female body relentlessly attempts to domesticate and emasculate the prototypical American male. He argues examples from Washington Irving to Ernest Hemingway:

> Ever since [Rip Van Winkle], the typical male protagonist of our fiction has been a man on the run, harried into the forest and out to sea, down the river or into combat—anywhere to avoid "civilization," which is to say, the confrontation of a man and woman which leads to the fall into sex, marriage, and responsibility. (26)

If this is the case, then men can only escape the power of women by continuing to overpower new tracts of virgin land. Anger at women who hold men back by their landed claims, reinscribing that hard fall "into sex, marriage, and responsibility" is a recurring motif in American literature and occurs, it seems, in "View." Although Mary's status as child and Mark's near-octogenarian status make the notion that she is trying to tie him to the land seem initially far-fetched, that is indeed what she is trying to do and is the reason he kills her—a particularly male form of rage, according to the symbol systems available. O'Connor wrote with a demonstrated awareness of this system. In the 1953 short story, "The Life You Save May Be Your Own," the tramp Tom T. Shiftlet informs Mrs. Crater of the differences between the stationary and the kinetic: "'A body and a spirit,' he repeated. 'The body, lady, is like a house: it don't go anywhere; but the spirit, lady, is like a automobile: always on the move, always'" (178).

By eliding body and house and land as one side of a Manichean dualism that makes all maleness movement and all spirit good while leaving everything that apparently opposes these to be evil, O'Connor creates a vexed gender economy that would certainly have recommended itself to the audience of Agrarian critics she needed to please. Quite likely, a masculinist readership enjoyed hearing that it was best, even most American—"See the

USA in your Chevrolet"—to be embodied male. Irene Diamond argues in *Fertile Ground: Women, Earth, and the Limits of Control* (1994) that "[m]ainstream Western feminism is still heavily implicated in the separation of mind from body and body from earth" (39). That is, women have dodged the oppressions of patriarchal exploitation by telling themselves that they are not embodied differently from males, except for a few reproductive organs, and that body does not matter anyway, only intellect and spirit. No matter the extent to which O'Connor consciously chose this attitude, evidence now abounds that her subconscious engaged with the issue quite differently. "A View of the Woods" bears out these engagements: in it, the body matters mightily.

"CAN'T STOP THE MARCHER TIME FOR A COW": BEARING LIKENESS

Mark Fortune wants the land to bear his likeness, and his likeness is "progressive": "He was not one of these old people who fight improvement, who object to everything new and cringe at every change" because progress "had always been his ally" (527). In bearing his likeness, the land will support pavement and a variety of commercial establishments meant to reflect this progress in its most up-to-date form—mobility: the gas station to fuel one's car; the motel, a newly-coined blend word to particularize it as a "hotel" for "motorists"; and a drive-in picture show, a specialized theater-going arrangement of the mid-twentieth century that foregrounds one's motoring life. Fortune's opening words, in fact, capture the dialectic between agrarian and progressive priorities: "'Any fool that would let a cow pasture interfere with progress is not on my books'" (525). And the fool in question would be Pitts, the son-in-law with no first name because Fortune does not bear him enough familial affection to call him by one. He is the "thin, long-jawed, irascible, sullen, sulking individual" who had married Fortune's daughter (527). Moreover, this female offspring has no salient features, not even a name: she is "his third or fourth daughter (he could never remember which)," and he makes no attempt to distinguish her because he does not "have any use for her" (526). The opening speech of the story argues both against agrarian values and against Mary Fortune Pitts's own "clay." Fortune likes to think of Mary "as being thoroughly of *his* clay" (528, my emphasis); but she does, in fact, embody her father in greater share than her maternal grandfather and is forced to carry this genetic assignment as if it were a manifestation of original sin.

In the opening moments of the scene, Mary shows herself jealous of the very dirt, a trait which rewards her grandfather's own allegiance to avarice. She also overlooks her grandfather having called her father a fool in preference to behavior that will be rewarded: she cautions her grandfather that the driver of the earthmover is about to "cut off some of your dirt!" (528). To make sure the gorging activity does not go beyond the stob, the child is "running along the edge of the embankment, her little yellow dress billowing out behind" (528). The yellow dress marks her as a double of the earthmoving machine, described as yellow at story's end. The edge along which she runs is the battle line between Mark Fortune and his son-in-law Pitts. Pitts's tenancy of the farmland is here the high ground; Fortune's siding with "progress"—in part to spite his son-in-law—is the excavated area that has created a bank. Old Fortune yells at her: "Don't run so near the edge" (528), fearing that she will fall. But the fall would be into the pit that he has created by his violent antagonism against his son-in-law Pitts, after he has been willing to pit father and daughter against one another. The "marcher time" that Fortune cannot stop is his own march toward the grave. His old age has brought him to the quiet desperation revealed by the brand of self-preserving "wisdom" upon which he bases his actions: "Anyone over sixty years of age is in an uneasy position unless he controls the greater interest" (526).

Mary bears up under "unmistakable likeness" at considerable cost. She was bartered to old Fortune at her conception. Like the first-born child promised to Rumpelstiltskin in order to allow the parents to continue enjoying the fruits of the earth, so too has Mary been traded for land rights. Ten years ago, the Pittses had come back to Mrs. Pitts's home to settle in with her father and work the family land. They had brought six children with them, a stalwart new generation of agrarians, only to discover that Mark Fortune planned to treat them not like family, but "like any other tenant[s]" (526). Appearing cold and self-serving in his dealings with them, the old man was no doubt transparent in his assessment of his daughter's circumstances: "She had married an idiot...and had seven children, all likewise idiots except the youngest, Mary Fortune, who was a throwback to him [Mark Fortune]. Pitts was the kind who couldn't keep his hands on a nickel [but who] had got to feel as if [he] owned the place" (526). But "ownership" of the place is merely the straightforward part of the struggle.

The Freudian underbelly is that Pitts has usurped the old man's daughter: "the old man considered that when she married Pitts she showed that she preferred Pitts to home" (526). The daughter's displacing the father to replace him with a husband creates a significant context for the current animosities. Fortune's retaliation is to put the betraying daughter in her place by assigning her mere tenant status. She responds by handing over their last-born child as a bribe for his favor. Without some legal claim to the farm they are farming, they cannot survive with any dignity, but only with his unloving largesse. They attempt to trade Mary for entitlement.

Once he sees her, Fortune wants her named Mary. Perhaps he yearns for his long-lost faith in both heavenly and earthly maternity: Mary as the mother of God and as the mother of Mark: "his beloved mother...had died seventy years ago, bringing him into the world" (527). His narcissism is stroked to find in this baby his replica: "short and broad like himself, with his very light blue eyes, his wide prominent forehead, his steady penetrating scowl and his rich florid complexion"; and that is not all: "she was like him on the inside too...had, to a singular degree, his intelligence, his strong will, and his push and drive" (526). Initially, Fortune had loudly declared that "he would put [his tenant relatives] off the place" if they dared "couple his name with the name Pitts" (527). Yet somehow he had relented when Mary had been born a girl—and one with an uncanny resemblance to him. In fact, he himself had suggested giving her his own mother's name when he saw "that even at the age of one day she bore his unmistakable likeness" (527). What he claimed then by claiming Mary was not Mary herself, but Mary himself, a Mary to serve as a bodily extension of the old man into a future that was, for him, all borrowed time. The year of her birth marked the year he had used up the last of his allocated threescore and ten. For the little girl, bearing his "unmistakable likeness" has meant bearing with his body that is too feeble to farm but still in need of companionship and with his vast egoism exacerbated by insecurity. She also bears the weight of his will to extend himself into a future by appropriating her fragile youth and innocence. A part of her innocence is the expectation of embrace by her own birth family. That denial, too, must be borne on the basis of unmistakable likeness. Because her grandfather likes her, her parents and siblings—his notion of "idiots"—cannot. Her affiliation with Mark Fortune, their scrooge of an unretiring patriarch, marks her as the enemy. This old "man of advanced vision" (528) cannot see his culpability in Mary Fortune's unfortunate alienation from every family member but him.

The second day into the time frame that opens with "the week before" finds the old man and Mary watching no longer an earthmover but "two huge yellow bulldozers," whose job, rather than gorging on the land, is smoothing it out (528). Mary, whom we first saw in a yellow dress, is still identified with the earth and with the yellow machines that shape it. But she has "a head of thick, very fine, sand-colored hair—the exact kind he [Fortune] had had when he had had any" (529). Hair that could have been yellow is instead sand-like, a mineral-world opposition to clay, perhaps that clay of his which she is "thoroughly of"—a salutary mixing that constitutes loaming soil far superior to either sand or clay alone. As this second round of watching unfolds, the narrator, positioned to watch us watching them, muses over one way in which the mirrored pair do *not* resemble each other: Mary's hair "grew straight and was cut just above her eyes and down the sides of her cheeks to the tips of her ears so that it formed a kind of door opening onto the central part of her face" (529). This door opens on the second day of the saga to reveal the horrors at the heart of this pastoral elegy.

In his musings, as Mary again walks the edge of the embankment, Mark thinks of the enlightened disciplinary methods he is able to use with her, a child with his own sort of sharp intelligence. He never lays a hand on her, even though he thinks the other six Pittses "should be whipped once a week on principle" (529). To Mary he offers capital. To induce her back from the edge, he chides: "'Remember what you won't get if you don't mind'" (529). What she ultimately will not get is the chance to live beyond age nine, beyond this week, but what Fortune eventually proves to be referencing here is a bonus: "he might be selling another lot soon and...if he did, he might give her a bonus but not if she gave him any sass" (531). Mary, giving him sass, replies that she "don't want no bonus" and "ain't ever...ask[ed] for one neither" and does not want her grandfather "buttin into [her] bidnis" (531). But none of this sort of sass bothers Mark Fortune: "He had frequent little verbal tilts with her but this was a sport like putting a mirror up in front of a rooster and watching him fight his reflection" (531). In other words, he sees no reason to discipline her for responding exactly as he would. It is, in fact, amusing to watch her give the same sharp-tongued responses to the world as he does.

What is less amusing is the extended flashback to disciplinary scenes of a violently different nature. Her father beats her. He displaces his anger at the repeated emasculations foisted upon him by his father-in-law onto Mark's "unmistakable likeness." With his "nasty temper" and "ugly unreasonable resentments," Pitts "[t]ime and again" gets up slowly from his place at the table (a side place because the old man still preserves the head for himself) and commands abruptly with a jerk of his head that Mary Fortune accompany him out of the room. He unfastens his belt as he goes (529–30). The terrifying incestuous grotesquerie of this dramatization serves to eroticize the beatings she then endures, even as Katherine Hemple Prown finds Mary's later death to be eroticized and likened to rape. These beatings frustrate Fortune. He in turn is emasculated in his ability to defend his double. The aggressions of the two men against each other meet in Mary. And Fortune especially hates the fact that she complies readily, almost eagerly, with her father's ruthless demands. Rather than sacrificial lamb or scapegoat, she becomes instead the contested terrain that, like the farm, her father will "whack" in order to possess.

"SOMETHING VERY LIKE COOPERATION"

Early in the story, Fortune has tried to protect Mary from falling over the edge of the embankment, and the narrator has supplied additional evidence of his zealous care for her safety: "He was always very careful to see that she avoided dangers. He would not allow her to sit in snakey places or put her hands on bushes that might hide hornets" (529). Evidently, he feels somewhat potent to protect her from natural dangers, but not from moral ones. When Pitts bids Mary leave the room with him, he drives her "down the road out of earshot" and silently, ritualistically beats her for three minutes while she clings to a pine tree: "Pitts, as methodically as if he were whacking a bush with a sling blade, beat her around the ankles with his belt" while she would "jump up and down as if she were standing on a hot stove and make a whimpering noise like a dog that was being peppered" (530). In this scene the symbolic use of Mary as the ground and grounding of warring natures is richly evidenced. She clings to the pine, the designated Christ figure, but neither man clings to the pine. Instead, an instinctual grasping after power drives each of them. Fortune wants Pitts's power to live and work in the virility of his vital years, but the younger, stronger man has already won the game: "Pitts knows that the best way to deal with a tyrant is to outlive him" (Giannone, *Hermit* 206). Pitts wants Fortune's legal title to the land so that his sweat over the acreage will not be wasted. He needs the land in order to provide for his family without being undermined by a hateful in-law at every turn. On the other hand, Fortune needs the land because he has been a hateful, idiot-calling in-law at every turn and so has no other way to preserve a place for himself. Even though Pitts is never described in favorable ways, James Mellard rules in his favor: Pitts,

> not old man Fortune [is] the exemplar of the law, of parental and Symbolic authority...a manifestation of that *lawful* authority of the parent over the child...the very arbitrariness of that authority and the child's acquiescence to it "prove" that Pitts has what the old man lacks, has the power of interdiction, the authority of the law of the name of the father. (637)

Each time Mary follows her father out to receive a beating, a "completely foreign" expression comes over her face that "infuriates" Old Fortune: "It was a look that was part terror and part respect and part something else, something very like cooperation" (530). She cooperates or submits to what she recognizes as the bargain these two patriarchs with authority over her body have struck. She pays *on her body* for every debt of land theft that Fortune commits against Pitts, the de facto authority over the property. Mark Fortune thinks that he supports the "marcher progress," but his whole project is to obstruct it in human terms. His era of rule is over. It passes to the new generation. Wishing to define himself as a man of "advanced vision," he is instead a man of advanced age who fears that the only move he has left is into the grave: "He knew they were waiting impatiently for the day when they could put him in a hole eight feet deep and cover him up with dirt" (527). Like old King David who wanted a youthful female body to warm him in his last days, Mark Fortune takes Mary as his Abishag: "Every morning since she had been able to climb, he had waked up to find her either on his bed or underneath it"; he expected to wake up "looking into a little red mirror framed in a door of fine hair" (539) or to find her "sitting astride his chest ordering him to make haste" to begin their day's adventures (535). And he will require her companionship relentlessly unto death.

"RIDING WITH THE WHORE OF BABYLON": SELLING OUT

When the twosome first "fell out" over the sale of the lawn, Mark had tried to argue Mary out of siding with her daddy by challenging her need to be loyal to someone who beat her, but she vehemently denied the beatings: "Nobody's ever put a hand on me and if anybody did, I'd kill him" (533). Fortune takes that as unwarranted support for a false god by calling her Jezebel, the Biblical wife of Ahab, who worshipped Baal: "Walk home by yourself. I refuse to ride a Jezebel!" (533). But Mary's retort is double-edged: "And I refuse to ride with the Whore of Babylon" (533). She is completely indifferent to his feeble comeback that "[a] whore is a woman!" and does not "deign to turn around" (533). She has said doubly true things. First, he has been emasculated in that his graceless lack of willingness to yield the farm to the next generation betrays an unmanly lack of courage. His cowardice takes the form of hiding behind Mary's "apron strings," letting her face beatings that should have been his. And such cowardice can be construed—in the binary oppositions of patriarchal currency—as weak and thereby as "womanly." Furthermore, he has sold himself, his birthright, and by extension, Mary to the highest bidder repeatedly, so he has indeed "whored" away the family's dignity.

In the third scene of "A View of the Woods" we are given the decisive action of the story, after the opening scenes have set up the Mary-to-Mark and Mary-to-Pitts framework. The two men cannot get at each other, except through Mary. When Pitts is beating Mary, old Fortune is "watching from behind a boulder about a hundred feet away" (530) too fearful of his heart condition to intervene, a heart condition that involves, as is frequently the case in O'Connor's fiction, something more than physical, requiring a treatment that is something more than medical. Fortune has just dropped on the family the climactic news: "he announced that noon at the dinner table that he was negotiating with a man named Tilman to sell the lot in front of the house for a gas station," causing his daughter to moan with despairing world-weariness "as if a dull knife were being turned slowly in her chest" and his six non-Mary grandchildren to begin "to bawl and pipe, 'Where we play!' 'Don't let him do that, Pa!' 'We won't be able to see the road!' and similar idiocies" (533). Mary, who had already attempted to dissuade the old man from this scheme, knows that the combined frustration and wrath of the other eight of her nuclear family members will soon be written on her body—and it is. Pitts turns to Mary with a "You done this to us" (534) and marches her off to the woods in a mode that is quite different from the "marcher progress." The "only pasture that Pitts had succeeded in getting the bitterweed off" was the parcel Fortune sold for a fishing resort (525). This new sale of the "two hundred feet from the road" that fronts the family home will make them physical prisoners, just as Fortune's land tyranny holds them economic prisoners (531). The lawn is—as Mary argued—where "daddy grazes his calves" (532) and where she and her siblings play, in addition to being their means to a view of the woods. This sale only strengthens her bond to Pitts. When he bids her to come as he unfastens his belt, "she slid away from the table and followed him, almost ran after him out the door and into the truck beside him" (534). Like lovers competing for the attentions of a coquette on the basis of their snazzy cars, her seat in her daddy's green truck is juxtaposed to her seat in and on old Mark's "battered mulberry-colored Cadillac" (525) as she rides by turns with each "lover" to assignations that lead always to violence. When she refuses to ride further with Mark Fortune, her daddy is there to pick her up, but then Mark Fortune lures her away in his Cadillac one last time, eventually driving her to her rendezvous with death.

Here is how the climactic scene evolves. Fortune disrupts his and Mary's celebration of progress—their box seats at the bulldozing scene—to keep an appointment with Tilman. Tilman's name, highly metaphorical like every other name in the story, converges a wealth of symbolism: as an entrepreneur, he has always an eye toward and a hand on the till; in play with the agrarian backdrop of the store, Tilman too digs up the land, but to erect monuments to progress, rather than to plant crops. His fields grow "old used-car bodies [and] outdoor ornaments, such as stone cranes and chickens, urns, jardinières, whirligigs, and farther back from the road, so as not to depress his dance-hall customers, a line of tombstones and monuments" (535). His business enterprises constitute a one-man show, as his ads leading up to the spot dramatically announce: "only five miles away, only four, only three, only two, only one: then 'Watch out for Tilman's, Around this bend!' and finally, 'Here it is, Friends, TILMAN'S!' in dazzling red letters" (535). Tilman's "combination country store, filling station, scrap-metal dump, used-car lot and dance hall" is the total amalgam of commercial progress; he even has "a barbeque pit" and sells "barbecued sandwiches and soft drinks" in his one-room structure (535). Locals can eat, drink, dance and be merry, gas up, and then lie right down and die. Tilman has the life cycle covered, turning a profit on every segment. And in addition to playing on his name, O'Connor plays on his looks:

> Tilman was a man of quick action and few words. He sat habitually with his arms folded on the counter and his insignificant head weaving snake-like fashion above them. He had a triangular-shaped face with the point at the bottom and the top of his skull was covered with a cap of freckles. His eyes were green and very narrow and his tongue was always exposed in his partly opened mouth. (542)

This snake-man element of Tilman allows a metaphoric replaying of the Garden of Eden, but Mary is no Eve.

Adamant against the temptation he offers, Mary is Eden itself, a plea for the preservation of the Law of the Father and for paradisiacal innocence. This day, she has been willing to ride with him to Tilman's because he keeps their destination a secret. Attempting, as is his habit, to coerce her good will with a bribe, he offers "I'll bring you something" when she gives "a sniffing look as if she scented an enemy" (536). But she deserts him. When he leaves his business conference after half an hour, she is not waiting in his car but has, according to the report of a "Negro boy, drinking a purple drink" outside the store, "gone off in a truck with a white man" (536). Her desertion foreshadows the larger desertion of their violent encounter. The narrative tone is indeed that of a jealous lover: "She had never left him before and certainly never for Pitts," the thought of which causes his feeling to race "between fury and mortification" (536). When he arrives home to find her "glum-faced" with "puffy and pink-rimmed" eyes, but with no marks from Pitts's belt, he tries to win her back: "He meant to make his voice severe but instead it came out crushed, as if it belonged to a suitor trying to reinstate himself" (537). But he cannot win her back. Her allegiance has not shifted simply to Pitts and the Law of the Father, but to the woods and its transcendent value, where she has a sense of her true country—"a gray-blue line of more distant woods and beyond that nothing but the sky, entirely blank except for one or two threadbare clouds" but somehow a scene so compelling that she stares at it "as if it were a person that she preferred to him" (537).

Following this unsuccessful interaction in which he finds her to be more Pitts than Fortune, much to his dismay, Mark spends the afternoon in his room, periodically rising from his bed to search the woods. It is the day that he encounters the "uncomfortable mystery" and has an uncomfortable dinner during which no one will speak to him; but just as Mary Fortune has a habit of talking to her feet, old Fortune talks to himself that evening for lack of a better companion. He lists the joys of having a Tilman establishment at the front door and hears "the throb of the future town of Fortune" underneath "the hum of crickets and tree frogs" (539). The next day, the last day of his and Mary's lives, she is not sitting across his chest when he awakens, but is already on the porch in communion with the woods. He tries to shake her mood by the offer of a trip to town. Promising that they will look for a boat to use at the new fishing resorts and make no other stops, she consents indifferently to going. But in fact, not the boat store, nor the offer of an ice cream cone nor even the dazzle of a visit to the ten-cent store with one of her grandfather's quarters to spend can wrest her from her bad humor. He then opts to do courthouse business since his "courting" has not worked, but he courts disaster by announcing that they will, after all, make one more stop. She has moved to the back seat during the interlude in which he was inside the government building having the deed and bill of sale prepared and will not speak to him when he reenters the car: "he might have been chauffeuring a small dead body for all the answer he got" (542). Since she is soon to be such a body, readers are forewarned: riding with the Whore of Babylon can kill you.

"THIS OUGHT TO TEACH YOU A GOOD LESSON": REAPING REMORSE

In the horrific scene that concludes "View," we find Mary throwing bottles at Tilman and Fortune as they conclude their business deal in "red-faced and wild-looking" hysteria—a gender-marked state of mind, she forces the erstwhile entrepreneurs to dodge her rapid-fire assaults. As her adrenalin rush subsides and he carries her to his old Cadillac, her emotions "spent," old Fortune decides to win back his masculine prowess and flagging authority by giving her a Pitts-style beating. Once in the woods, however, she chooses not to grab the tree and submit, but to grab her grandfather and launch into a set of hands-on assaults: blows with her fists, pummeling, growling, battering, pounding, kicks into his stomach and crotch, and bites into the side of his jaw (544–45). Allowing him to catch his breath when he pleads that he is not only an "old man" but also her grandfather, she mirrors the same kind of "sass" he has enacted and applauded throughout the story. She brags, "You have been whipped...by me...and I'm PURE Pitts" (545). As critics from Sister Kathleen Feeley and Frederick Asals to Susan Morrow Paulson and John Roos have explained, the old man cannot countenance being vanquished by the Pitts elements of himself or his double. Being a Pitts carries the "disgust" of being "completely defeated" (541), as his shadow self has always feared he actually is or soon would be. So he rolls over onto his granddaughter with "his hands still tight around her neck" and lifts up her head to bring it "down once hard against the rock that happened to be under it," and then he brings it down "twice more" so that when the eyes "slowly rolling back, appear not to pay him the slightest attention," he can say in hollow triumph, "'There's not an ounce of Pitts in me'" (545). His moves in this scene, moves that Katherine Prown rightly deems "eroticized," are like those of a lover whose impassioned strokes are intended to bring on what Victorians delicately termed "a little death," but here they bring on actual death—and for a similar reason. They are the strokes of eros upon "the supremely high valuation each ego secretly assigns itself" (Updike 233). That old Mark has destroyed the body of his "lover"—the female he hoped to recreate narcissistically as a version of himself—is a fitting conclusion to a story in which he is hellbent on destroying his land.

A. R. Coulthard once deemed "A View of the Woods" a "view of the worst" that O'Connor had written, finding neither Mark nor Mary empathetic enough as characters for us to care about their deaths (8). Sister Bertrande Meyers thought it best that Mary Fortune did not live longer because, with her grandfather as mentor, she was likely to have grown ever more unlovely: "What she might have become a few years more under the devastating tutelage of old Mark Fortune is unpleasant and unnecessary to contemplate" (424). Yet Mary Fortune Pitts shows a heroic nature that few O'Connor characters ever exhibit. If we consider her to embody the Edenic virgin land, then we might choose to take the parallel one step further and see her as both a form of the Promised Land—another sort of Eden—and the deliverer of the Pitts family to it. In other words, she is, as Sister Bertrande herself first saw, a Moses figure. Moses, favored by Pharaoh and chosen as his associate and heir, is also given his name (424). The Pittses behave like the Israelites in their "fleeing at last from a bondage no longer endurable, coming finally under the guidance of Moses to the promised land—a land which he, like his little prototype, Mary Fortune, died without seeing" (424). While the Pittses do not flee from bondage, strictly speaking, they do rankle ever harder against it until Mary gives up her privileged status as Pharaoh's chosen one and takes their part. Mary, in turn fleeing her role as the oppressor's associate, puts herself in mortal danger. Pharaoh's attempt to block the Israelites from at-one-ment with their true country centered on killing their children, children as the ground on which civilizations are built, that elemental energy that generates the generations and legacies of families.

Even Harold Bloom, a preeminent literary arbiter of our day, finds Mary as unattractive as her grandfather: "I am uncertain which of the two is the more abominable moral character or hideous human personality, partly because they resemble one another so closely in selfishness, obduracy, false pride, sullenness, and just plain meanness" (5). But Bloom, Meyers, and Coulthard simply sell Mary short. Her grandfather may be quite the quintessential O'Connor egotist, and he may have attempted to stamp out in Mary all that did not bear his own progressive stamp, but O'Connor proves his values and choices to have been dead wrong, while she shows Mary Fortune Pitts to be dead, but not wrong. As James Mellard demonstrates, Mark exploits Mary only as long as she gratifies his vanity, once she "manifest[s] a contrary determination to ally herself with the father—Pitts—and thus with the Name of the Father (theologically, God; psychoanalytically, the Other), she no longer satisfies old man Fortune's indentificatory narcissistic needs" (640).

The Biblical symbol system at work in the story is richly cross-wired. In fact, this is so much the case that Terry Eagleton's definition of the grotesque helps explain it. The grotesque, writes Eagleton, is an "intrinsically double-faced, an immense semiotic switchboard through which codes are read backwards and messages scrambled into their antithesis" (145). The immense semiotic switchboard that entangles Mark and Mary as participants in a legacy of living embodiments that are necessarily landed, whether in the pastoral or the progressive mode, is as intricate and intense as any narrative O'Connor ever created. This makes A. R. Coulthard's view that "View" is "the only story in [her] two collections which totally fails either to delight or instruct…her worst piece of fiction" (7) his "worst" moment as a critic. For surely "View" is among her best pieces of fiction—the entanglement of generations, enacting the charged and intimate drama of family life and its legacy, a study in who wrests power from whom when, on what terms, and to what end. And Mary, who overcomes exploitation, lays down her life for and as a part of the land that she knows intuitively to be a means to the transcendent, her—and her family's and our own—true country.

WORKS CITED

Bloom, Harold. *Flannery O'Connor: Modern Critical Views*. New York: Chelsea House, 1986.

Burt, Daniel S. *The Literary 100: A Ranking of the Most Influential Novelists, Playwrights, and Poets of All Time*. New York: Checkmark, 2001.

Byrd, William. *Histories of the Dividing Line Betwixt Virginia and North Carolina*. Ed. William K. Boyd. Raleigh, NC: Historical Commission, 1929.

Cooper, James Fenimore. *The Prairie: A Tale. The Works of James Fenimore Cooper*. Vol. 5 New York: G. P. Putnam's Sons, 1893.

Coulthard, A. R. "Flannery O'Connor's 'A View of the Woods': A View of the Worst." *Notes on Contemporary Literature* 17.1 (January 1987): 7-9.

Diamond, Irene. *Fertile Ground: Women, Earth, and the Limits of Control*. Boston: Beacon, 1994.

Eagleton, Terry. *Walter Benjamin, or Towards a Revolutionary Criticism*. London: Verso, 1981.

Fiedler, Leslie. *Love and Death in the American Novel*. 1960. New York: Bantam Doubleday, 1966.

Fitzgerald, F. Scott. *The Great Gatsby: The Authorized Text*. Ed. Matthew Bruccoli. New York: Simon & Schuster-Scribner, 1991.

Giannone, Richard. "Displacing Gender: Flannery O'Connor's View from the Woods." *Flannery O'Connor: New Perspectives*. Ed. Sura P. Rath and Mary Neff Shaw. Athens: U of Georgia P, 1996. 73–95.

———. *Flannery O'Connor: Hermit Novelist*. Urbana: U of Illinois P, 2000.

Kolodny, Annette. *The Lay of the Land: Metaphor as Experience and History in American Life*. Chapel Hill: U of North Carolina P, 1975.

Mellard, James M. "Flannery O'Connor's Others: Freud, Lacan, and the Unconscious."*American Literature* 61.4 (1989): 625–43.

Meyers, Bertrande. "Four Stories of Flannery O'Connor." *Thought: A Review of Culture and Idea*. 37.146 (September 1962): 410–26.

O'Connor, Flannery. *Collected Works*. Ed. Sally Fitzgerald. New York: Library of America, 1988.

———. *The Habit of Being*. Ed. Sally Fitzgerald. New York: Farrar, Straus and Giroux, 1979.

———. *Mystery and Manners: Occasional Prose*. Ed. Sally Fitzgerald and Robert Fitzgerald. New York: Farrar, Straus and Giroux, 1969.

Prown, Katherine Hemple. *Revising Flannery O'Connor: Female Authorship and the Southern Literary Tradition*. Charlottesville: UP of Virginia, 2001.

Smith, Lillian. *Killers of the Dream*. New York: Norton, 1949.

Twain, Mark. *Adventures of Huckleberry Finn: An Authoritative Text, Contexts and Sources, Criticism.* 3rd ed. Ed. Thomas Cooley. New York: Norton, 1999.

Updike, John. "More Love in the Western World." *Assorted Prose*. Knopf: Fawcett Crest, 1966. 220–33.

Yaeger, Patricia. "Flannery O'Connor and the Aesthetics of Torture." *Flannery O'Connor: New Perspectives*. Athens: U of Georgia P, 1996. 183–206.

Survival in a Patriarchal World

J. JUNE SCHADE

What purpose does the feministic reevaluation of literature serve for those who seek the knowledge that such an undertaking could potentially reveal? As women, it has become vitally important for us to reestablish our place in society, both historically and culturally, as valuable contributors to that society. If we can, through reevaluation, discern a more accurate understanding of our past, we will most certainly find ourselves better prepared for our present and for that which lies ahead (Grosz 1018). We must develop our "feminist history" which will equip us to move forward as women and with which we shall discover new perspectives on which our future is based (Grosz 1019). For this considerable endeavor it has become essential that we rethink our literary history, not just as human beings but as women, in order that we may better understand ourselves, our history, our present and our future. "In this sense," states Elizabeth Grosz, "the astute feminist historian stands on the cusp of the folding of the past into the future, beyond the control or limit of the present" (1019). It is especially important for theorists who are revisiting writers not typically considered part of the feminist literary category to search well to ensure that all those who deserve recognition as contributors to feminism as it has now come to be known are counted.

Until recently, the Southern writer Flannery O'Connor, has been largely ignored by feminist theory and criticism, though some scholars have begun to assert O'Connor's undeniable feminist contribution. It is with the feminist critical conclusions of these individuals regarding O'Connor's work and her indisputable feminism that I intend to add my voice. Too often, O'Connor's critics have insisted that, in conjunction with her conventionalism, her conservatism and her Catholicism (Spivey 9), her negative portrayal of women and the feminine in her work are convincing proof of the unsympathetic and patriarchal viewpoint O'Connor held concerning women. However, the brutal treatment of women in her fiction became a necessary element in each story in order to fully demonstrate the level to which the position of women had deteriorated. O'Connor's fiction, according to Ted R. Spivey "takes into full account the suffering endured by...women...in a Southern culture whose hierarchy had become...extremely rigid" (60–61).

Yet, this subjugation of the feminine in O'Connor's work does not signify any allegiance to the male hierarchy; rather, conversely, it illustrates how scrupulously she viewed the patriarchy and parodied its rigorous characteristics to reveal its devastating flaws.

The analysis of Flannery O'Connor's fiction from a feminist standpoint has been severely limited due, in part, to the restricted scope within which most of her work was critiqued, but also because of scholarly research done from an undeniably masculine, more specifically, Catholic viewpoint. Contrary to the opinions of such critics, O'Connor's subjugative literary depiction of women within her narratives validates her status as a feminist, and more specifically, a cultural feminist. "A cultural theory," according to Elaine Showalter, "acknowledges that there are important differences between women as writers: class, race, nationality, and history are literary determinates as significant as gender" ("Feminist Criticism" 63). O'Connor recognized the complexity of the cultural history of the southern regions of the United States, especially for women, and believed that "[t]he best American fiction has always been regional" (*Mystery and Manners* 58). O'Connor's fiction directly reflects those unique "literary determinates" from within the region where she lived (Showalter, "Feminist Criticism" 63) as O'Connor utilized her own rich experiences and keen perceptions as a southern woman to accurately depict the plight of the feminine in the South.

Flannery O'Connor crafted her fiction in such a way so as to best amplify the powerful, yet increasingly antiquated patriarchal hierarchy being imposed upon women in the South at this time. For she indeed recognized the tenuous place the South occupied when she wrote: "The present state of the South is one wherein nothing can be taken for granted, one in which our identity is obscured and in doubt" (*Mystery and Manners* 57). O'Connor's acknowledgment of the precarious state of the South is explicitly linked to her deep awareness of the need for a change in the ways in which women were viewed and ultimately treated.

Stemming from the regional instability she was privy to, O'Connor incorporated into her fiction what she considered to be the fundamental flaws affecting the social hierarchy in the South, including the continuous slide—even potential disappearance—of traditional family values, the predicament of children in the wake of this crumbling values system, and the complete inability of men in the South to find successful solutions for their communities' elemental financial dilemmas: all of which ultimately led to the necessity of women assuming roles in society for which they were neither traditionally expected to perform, nor which they were adequately prepared to undertake (Spivey 2–3). In demonstrating the significance of the aforementioned issues to O'Connor, it becomes increasingly clear that her concerns fell decidedly outside of the masculine mainstream then in vogue. During the same period that O'Connor documented these problems in her fiction (Spivey 11), the civil rights and feminist movements were rippling throughout the South bringing cries for racial and sexual equality increasingly closer to Andalusia, O'Connor's home outside Milledgeville, Georgia. With these cries came the demand for the entire country, not just the Southern regions, to reassess their traditional values systems (Mee 1). Flannery O'Connor, in typical visionary style, foresaw the forthcoming changes. Unhappily, she also anticipated the difficult struggle that lay ahead for those who rallied for change, recognizing the limitations surrounding the movement within the South and also in her own ability, as a woman, a Southerner, and a writer, to bring about change (Gentry 62). However, this did not extinguish O'Connor's hope for a better future and, according to one of her closest friends, Maryat Lee, "[O'Connor] shared with [her] the sense of frustration...over the dilemma of the...South"; but, unlike many involved with the Civil Rights movement, O'Connor did not place any confidence in the dramatic tactics employed too often by its 'activists,' placing her hopes in a gradual, less disruptive process (*Habit of Being* 193), perhaps to allow Southerners the opportunity to adjust to a new way of thinking after long years of living in the vicious circle of consummate patriarchal dominance.

The fiction that Flannery O'Connor crafted was her contribution to the gradual change she so hoped for in the South. The struggles that arose in O'Connor's fiction were coarse and sprung from her astute examination and final determination of what it meant to be either man or woman in 'conservative, patriarchal southern families' (Giannone 80). Accordingly, it would not be impossible to imagine that O'Connor's unflattering portrayal of the South was her technique as a woman writer, much like Virginia Woolf's in her essays, of illustrating the system of patriarchal authority in order to expose its "contradictions" (Fisher 32). O'Connor documented the lives of ordinary people, people who were her neighbors, her community members, and even her family members with the intention of illustrating the differences in race, class, and gender especially germane to the region. These people found their way onto the pages of O'Connor's fiction—together with those everyday details she viewed as mundane—in order that those same people who read her stories could relate to the particular circumstances in each and identify a part of themselves, whether socially or emotionally, in her stories.

For O'Connor, "[f]iction [was] about everything human" (*Mystery and Manners* 68). Her stories were not about subjects or places she could not fathom. With her guidance, the fiction she crafted became three-dimensional. O'Connor created each story with the belief that the characters she gave life to, the words they spoke and the circumstances in which they inevitably found themselves were "indissolubly" connected to reality, a view that many feminists share with O'Connor (Giannone 93).

Yet, reality in O'Connor's writing encompassed a great many ideals. The South into which Flannery O'Connor was born and raised held a disconcerting viewpoint of women due, for the most part, to its traditional male-dominated hierarchy. In her fiction, O'Connor was able to explore the different manifestations of power struggles that occurred within the established hierarchy (Westling 111). Moreover, though many of O'Connor's stories include familiar single mother/daughter scenarios, she utilized an undeniable, repeated male dominance in her fiction to expose the "insufficiency" of such dominance, allowing her stories to become testimonials to women by uncovering within them an inevitable "sexual violence" which many feminists believe to be at the root of the patriarchal hierarchy (Westling, "Fathers and Daughters" 121).

For example, in "The Life You Save May Be Your Own," Lucynell Crater and her namesake daughter are O'Connor's familial pair whose independence goes unquestioned and unchallenged as they have managed the farm, though humbly without the assistance of a male figure for over fifteen years. Until this moment, they had need for no other person than each other. However, the atmosphere quickly changes with the entrance and presence of the one-armed tramp, Mr. Tom T. Shiftlet (145). In O'Connor's fiction, according to Josephine Hendin, "men are either old, asleep, dead, diseased, or mutilated, or murderers and thieves" (qtd. in Rath and Shaw 68). The image of this man with his half limb can certainly be seen as intentional in an attempt to diminish his effectiveness as the masculine force in the story. Yet, even in the presence of this "mutilated" man, by their very involvement with him, these female "pretensions" of independence begin to slip away, eventually dissolving entirely, leaving both mother and daughter vulnerable (Paulson 198). The older woman finds opportunity in Shiftlet's arrival, envisioning the future possibility of a son-in-law with all of its benefits. In Shiftlet's visual appraisal of the Crater property, including Lucynell, Jr., and the dilapidated Ford, he also sees future possibilities. Unfortunately, their separate visions do not create a final, whole picture, and the tramp seizes ultimate control of the situation, despite his physical lack—perhaps because both Mr. Shiftlet and Mrs. Crater have each been conditioned by their collective cultural history to believe that by the simple virtue of his maleness he should and will prevail.

O'Connor subtly shifts the power between the male and female roles when her illustration of the patriarchal hierarchy begins to reveal its underlying contradictions. Though the owner of the farm and the person for whom Mr. Shiftlet goes to work, Mrs. Crater submits to Shiftlet in an attempt to secure a marriage vow for her daughter. O'Connor effectively utilizes the power reversal in order to demonstrate how, within the established patriarchal society and in the presence of masculinity, no matter how ill-formed, women are expected to conform to that which is believed to be an acceptable female role, severely limiting their control and their contribution to their community, as well as limiting their own "self" (Paulson 29). Critic Claire Kahane has accused Flannery O'Connor of "a repugnance towards femaleness" (qtd. in Paulson 30). However, if Kahane's assertion regarding O'Connor is correct that she sympathized more with the masculine than with the feminine, why would O'Connor consistently portray male characters in such a demoralizing and defeating way unless she was attempting to reveal a much larger and darker truth about the society in which she lived?

Likewise, O'Connor frequently utilizes the afflicted female body. Due to the association of the female and/or of femininity with the physical body, any reference to a woman's physique, especially if afflicted or distorted in some way, becomes another tactic by which to further distinguish and degrade women (Reesman 44). In addition to the tramp's half-limb, the distorted body also manifests itself in Mrs. Crater's daughter, Lucynell, Jr. She is "completely deaf" and consequently mute until Mr. Shiftlet, in an attempt to befriend and gain the young woman's trust, teaches her to say "bird" (150). O'Connor describes this woman as "innocent", meant literally to be interpreted as virginal, and Mrs. Crater uses her daughter's unspoiled body as a bargaining tool with which to manipulate Mr. Shiftlet into taking a marriage vow (151–52). Her deafness becomes especially pertinent in conjunction with Elaine Showalter's assertion that, "the woman writer [is urged] to ally herself with everything in the culture which is muted, silenced, or unrepresented, in order to subvert the existing systems" (Introduction 9). Her inability to communicate until Mr. Shiftlet appears could be argued as

O'Connor's way of revealing how woman has been silenced except for what man has taught her to say and how, by direct virtue of the limited roles warranted by the particular cultural and historical period, they have been taken advantage of by the male hierarchy (Calhoun 68).

The acts of violence in "The Life You Save May Be Your Own" occur against both Mrs. Crater and her daughter, though Lucynell, Jr. undoubtedly will suffer more than her mother. Once married, Mr. Shiftlet takes Lucynell, Jr. away from her mother's farm, presumably for the first time in her life, and much to Mrs. Crater's sorrow. However, once Lucynell, Jr. is asleep on the counter of The Hot Spot, Mr. Shiftlet tells the young man working she is only a hitchhiker and he deserts her. At the end of the story O'Connor leaves much undone; she does not say what happens to the girl or whether she ever makes it home to the Crater farm. Though O'Connor does make it clear that both women have suffered immeasurably for their brief acquaintance with Mr. Shiftlet, by leaving their fates unwritten, she allows for the possibility of female perseverance, especially during the concluding moments when Mr. Shiftlet suffers from a sudden and overwhelming sense of guilt, "that the rottenness of the world was about to engulf him" (156).

The definitive loss of feminine independence, the debasement of women through the use of the afflicted female body, and the possibility of feminine perseverance found in this story can also be found in other stories—"Good Country People" and "A Circle in the Fire" are two that readily come to mind—but these are only some of the common traits O'Connor uses to illustrate a contradictory hierarchy. O'Connor also frequently portrays figurative or literal violence enacted upon the feminine by the dominating male presence in its last attempt to assure, once and for all, its authority. Through these acts of violence, O'Connor portrays 'the carrion of misogyny' (Giannone 93), arguably in order to demonstrate how the traditional patriarchal hierarchy has encouraged the continued and unbridled abuse of women in the face of the traditional male's own "thinly veiled contempt" for the submissive, helpless females who are simply the monsters of their master's arrogant creation (Friedan 87).

As the foregoing essays attest, Flannery O'Connor's feministic tendencies can readily be found in the pages of her fiction. The way in which O'Connor approached her writing can best be described, "as [an] insider-outsider" (Spivey 88). As an "insider" O'Connor portrayed the dominant male attitudes in her writing, creating a reality in her stories which paralleled the reality of the South. However, as an "outsider" O'Connor was still a woman; she felt very strongly about being a woman and believed that it was her duty to explore the "role of the feminine in life" (Spivey 88–89), an exploration directly reflected in her work.

The female characters in O'Connor's fiction are not unfeminine, in fact, they are quite feminine, but they adopt certain masculine traits out of necessity in order to ensure that their farms, their homes, and their families survive in communities where their femininity is not just taken for granted, but very much abused (Smith 35–36). O'Connor's fiction demonstrates how these women endure, despite the overwhelming reality that the patriarchal system will prevail. She also demonstrates the absurdity of a system based upon an unwritten "creed" which necessitated that the ideal woman be submissive, and disallows for any valuable contribution to be made by these women to their communities (Gordon 114–15). It was, in fact, during this period that women were deeply involved within the workings of society because that society lacks decent male counterparts who could adequately perform the duties being assumed by women. Flannery O'Connor's fiction does not glorify the dominance of the male hierarchy; instead O'Connor exploits the feminine in order to expose how women have historically been mishandled. Through her fiction, O'Connor creates a voice for those who felt as she did that the end of the dominating patriarchal hierarchy in the South, indeed in the entire country, was drawing to its inevitable conclusion.

A reassessment of the fiction of Flannery O'Connor reveals an undeniable feministic quality to her work. Though the methods employed by O'Connor to illustrate the antiquated social system that she, and many other generations of women had endured, were certainly unorthodox by many feminists' standards, the anticipated result for women remained intact. However, the research regarding O'Connor's feministic vision is limited, and if we are ever to truly understand the full complexity of Flannery O'Connor, the writer, the Southerner, and the woman, then our work has only just begun.

WORKS CITED

Calhoun, Cheshire. "Thinking about the Plurality of Gender." *Hypatia* 16 (Spring 2001): 67–74. EBSCOHOST. Roosevelt University Library, Schaumburg. 26 September 2002.

Fisher, Jane Elizabeth. "The Seduction of the Father: Virginia Woolf and Leslie Stephen." *Women's Studies* 18 (1990): 31–48. EBSCOHOST. Roosevelt University Library, Schaumburg. 22 October 2002.

Friedan, Betty. *The Feminine Mystique*. New York: Norton, 1997.

Gentry, Marshall Bruce. "Gender Dialogue in O'Connor." Rath and Shaw 62–68.

Giannone, Richard. "Displacing Gender: Flannery O'Connor's View from the Woods." Rath and Shaw 80–93.

Grosz, Elizabeth. "Histories of a Feminist Future." *Signs: Journal of Women in Culture and Society* 25 (Summer 2000): 1017–1021. EBSCOHOST. Roosevelt University Library, Schaumburg. 22 October 2002.

Gordon, Sarah. "'The Crop': Limitation, Restraint and Possibility." Rath and Shaw 96–120.

Mee, Susie, ed. *An Anthology of Southern Women Writers*. San Diego: Harcourt, 1995.

O'Connor, Flannery. *The Complete Stories*. New York: Farrar, Straus and Giroux, 1973.

———. *The Habit of Being*. Ed. Sally Fitzgerald. New York: Farrar, Straus and Giroux, 1979.

———. *Mystery and Manners*. Ed. Sally Fitzgerald and Robert Fitzgerald. New York: Farrar, Straus and Giroux, 1969.

Paulson, Suzanne Morrow. *Flannery O'Connor: A Study of the Short Fiction*. Boston: Twayne Publishers, 1988.

Rath, Sura P., and Mary Neff Shaw. *Flannery O'Connor: New Perspectives*. Athens: UP of Georgia, 1996.

Reesman, Jeanne Campbell. "Women, Language and the Grotesque in Flannery O'Connor and Eudora Welty." Rath and Shaw 41–44.

Showalter, Elaine. "Feminist Criticism in the Wilderness." *Contemporary Literary Criticism: Literary and Cultural Studies*. Ed. Robert Con Davis and Ronald Schleifer. New York: Longman, 1994. 51–71.

———. Introduction. *The New Feminist Criticism*. Ed. Elaine Showalter. New York: Pantheon Books, 1985. 3–17.

Smith, Peter A. "Flannery O'Connor's Empowered Women." *Southern Literary Journal* 26 (Spring 1994): 35–47. EBSCOHOST. Roosevelt University Library, Schaumberg. 22 October 2002.

Spivey, Ted R. *Flannery O'Connor: The Woman, the Thinker, the Visionary*. Macon: Mercer UP, 1995.

Westling, Louise. "Fathers and Daughters in Welty and O'Connor." *The Female Tradition in Southern Literature*. Ed. Carol S. Manning. Urbana: UP of Illinois, 1993. 111–21.

Contributors

Christine Atkins has published essays on the issues of rape and violence in women's literature in *Women's Studies: An Interdisciplinary Journal, Concerns: The Journal of the Women's Caucus of the MLA,* and *Journal x: A Journal in Culture and Criticism.* Also a published poet, she teaches at Queensborough Community College in Queens, New York.

Margaret D. Bauer, author of *The Fiction of Ellen Gilchrist*, is editor of the *North Carolina Literary Review*. She has published articles on Southern writers in *Mississippi Quarterly, Southern Literary Journal, Studies in Short Fiction, College Literature, College Language Association Journal, Pembroke Magazine* and *Southern Studies.* Her essays also appear in *Critical Essays on Kate Chopin, Ellen Glasgow: New Perspectives,* and *Critical Essays on Alice Walker.* She teaches at East Carolina University in Greenville, North Carolina.

Robert Donahoo is the editor of *Cheers!: The Flannery O'Connor Society Newsletter.* He has published on Flannery O'Connor's fiction in *Literature and Belief, The Journal of Contemporary Thought, CEA Critic, Journal of the Short Story in English,* and *The Flannery O'Connor Bulletin.* His other publications include articles and essays on subjects including Tolstoy's novel, *Resurrection,* the drama of Horton Foote, and Postmodern American Science Fiction. He served as the book review editor for *The Texas Review* from 1995–2000. He teaches English at Sam Houston State University in Huntsville, Texas.

Marshall Bruce Gentry is the author of *Flannery O'Connor's Religion of the Grotesque.* He has also published on Flannery O'Connor and her work in *Flannery O'Connor: New Perspectives, Realist of Distances: Flannery O'Connor Revisited, The Flannery O'Connor Bulletin, Cheers!: The Flannery O'Connor Society Newsletter, The Southern Quarterly,* and *Modern Fiction Studies.* He is Editor of the *Flannery O'Connor Review* and Professor of English at Georgia College & State University.

Avis Hewitt has published essays in such collections as *Twenty-Four Ways of Looking at Mary McCarthy* and *John Updike and Religion*, as well as essays on Denise Levertov and John Updike in *Renascence* and *Christianity and Literature*. She teaches English at Grand Valley State University in Allendale, Michigan.

Dawn Keetley, co-editor of the three-volume *Public Women, Public Words: A Documentary History of American Feminism,* has published articles and book reviews on American literature and women's literature in *Legacy: A Journal of American Women Writers, American Quarterly, American Transcendental Quarterly, and ESQ: Emerson Society Quarterly*. She serves as Vice-President of the Society for the Study of American Women Writers, as a member of the advisory board for *Legacy*, and as a reader for *ESQ*. She teaches English at Lehigh University in Bethlehem, Pennsylvania.

J. June Schade is currently a graduate student in English at Roosevelt University in Chicago, Illinois. Her research interests include nineteenth and twentieth century American women's fiction, Southern women's literature, and gender roles and sexuality.

Natalie Wilson recently completed her doctorate at the University of London, Birkbeck College. She has published articles in *The International Journal of Gender and Sexuality*, *Xchanges*, and *Scope*, and has essays forthcoming in two collections entitled *Butler Matters* and *Ingestation.*

Virginia Wray edited *Cheers!: The Flannery O'Connor Society Newsletter* from its first issue in 1992 to 2002. She has published on Flannery O'Connor's fiction in *The Flannery O'Connor Bulletin, Renascence, The Antagonish Review, Publications of the Arkansas Philological Association,* and *English Language Notes.* Her work has frequently focused on O'Connor's juvenilia, master's thesis, and third unfinished novel *Why Do the Heathen Rage?* She is Professor of English and Coordinator of Academic Support Services at Lyon College in Batesville, Arkansas.